The Quotable Writer

Also Edited by Lamar Underwood

Classic Hunting Stories
Classic War Stories
The Greatest Adventure Stories Ever Told
The Greatest Disaster Stories Ever Told
The Greatest Fishing Stories Ever Told
The Greatest Flying Stories Ever Told
The Greatest Hunting Stories Ever Told
The Greatest Survival Stories Ever Told
The Greatest War Stories Ever Told
Into the Backing
Man Eaters
The Quotable Soldier
Theodore Roosevelt on Hunting
True Tales of the Mountain Men
Whitetail Hunting Tactics of the Pros

The Quotable Writer

Edited and with an Introduction
by Lamar Underwood

THE LYONS PRESS
Guilford, Connecticut
An imprint of The Globe Pequot Press

The Lyons Press is an imprint of The Globe Pequot Press.

10 9 8 7 6 5 4 3 2 1

Printed in the United States of America

Library of Congress Cataloging-in-Publication Data

The quotable writer / edited and with an introduction by Lamar Underwood.
      p. cm.
  Includes bibliographical references and index.
   ISBN 1-59228-133-8 (trade cloth)
  1. Authorship--Quotations, maxims, etc. 2. Authors--Quotations. I. Underwood, Lamar.
PN165.Q68 2004
808'.02--dc22

                                    2004004015

DEDICATED
TO
NICK LYONS

Publisher, Editor, Writer, Professor,
Husband, Father, Soldier, Angler
...and Friend of Writers Everywhere

His door has never been closed, and the lights within never
turned off.

CONTENTS

Acknowledgments

The unselfish, steadfast dedication of Lyons Press Holly Rubino to bringing this book from idea, to manuscript, to printed page is gratefully acknowledged. Without her assistance, the book would not be the same—and by that I mean to say that it would not be as good, or perhaps not even exist at all.

—Lamar Underwood

Introduction

So you want to be a writer. Or perhaps your interest in writing and writers is more of a scholarly nature—to teach or to simply satisfy personal curiosities about the writing life.

Imagine, if you will, finding yourself in the middle of a dream-like, fantasy cocktail party, within earshot of writers, editors, publishers, and agents whose every word you long to hear. There's Norman Mailer, talking trash to Tom Wolfe and Gore Vidal. Maxwell Perkins is speaking quietly to a clutch of people about editing Ernest Hemingway, F. Scott Fitzgerald, Thomas Wolfe, and James Jones. Novelist and screenwriter William Goldman is talking story and plot with the noted teacher and *Story* writer, Robert McKee. The room is packed to overflowing with rich and famous masters of the writing arts, and their comments about their ideas and experiences are floating through the room with the intensity of critical messages you feel destined to receive. You're picking up wonderful stuff—tips, insights, do's and don'ts.

Then, suddenly, you wake up. The dream is gone.

You, the aspiring writer, are back where you started. Alone and lonely. Alone with your intense desire to become a successful writer, to find your way through the maze and entanglements of the painful learning experiences, the rejections, the crushing walls of obscurity. How did they do it, those godlike figures whose books, plays, and films are icons of success? Is it all tricks? Secrets that they know and you don't? *Making It.* That's what it's all about. What must you do, what must you know, to find your own path to selling what you write and being read and appreciated? Easy answers to these questions are hard to find. And your search is usually a lonely one, for there are few loved-ones and friends who can discuss your work with what you desperately need—knowledge and compassion.

You, the wannabe writer, resourceful teacher, or curious bystander: Welcome to my party. In the pages that follow, I have attempted to bring together, in one convenient place, some of the most interesting and meaningful quotes ever uttered or written about writing and the writing life. If this book does not inspire, delight, or prove useful to you in some way, I shall be deeply disappointed.

There is a wonderful quote by the nature writer, Ernest Thompson Seton, that goes: "Because I have known the agonies of thirst, I would dig a well so that others might drink." Although my situation is not quite that dramatic, I am at the stage in life when I can look back very clearly and recall the difficulties and struggles of a young man wanting to succeed as a writer and editor. Guideposts and maps for such literary ambitions were few and far between. Back then, in the 1950s, *Writer's Digest* and *The Writer* were around, but not many good books in which the pros shared the do's and don'ts of their exclusive worlds. One picked one's way through biographies and autobiographies to glean whatever insider "secrets" one could, and trusted in teachers and the two aforementioned magazines to round out one's education and training. Today, unless you've been living on Mars, you know the library, bookstore shelves, and Internet sites to be filled with excellent books on writing and editing everything from term papers to screenplays. It is this editor's hope that this little volume will add a valuable title to this precious list of guides for writers and teachers.

It may be hard to imagine that a simple quote from another writer, perhaps from decades or even centuries before our time, can be meaningful to a writer or teacher of today. But trust me: This is exactly the case. Some quotes literally—forgive me—go for the jugular with illuminating insight on common, troublesome writing disorders and dilemmas. Hemingway, for instance, describes one piece of advice as "the most important thing I can tell you so try to remember it." Now we all know Papa wasn't exactly shy when it came to letting people know what he thought—particularly after he'd had a few belts—but "the most important thing"? One can't help but want to know the answer to this—and, no, I'm not going to spoil it by trying to tell you here.

One of the most interesting aspects of the quotes to me personally is the number of cases where the advice given is contradictory from one writer to the next. The astute reader will find this to be particularly evident in the highly mysterious region of plotting.

For every writer of fiction, especially in the case of the novel, who begins the journey into the story with a clear and firm idea of where the book is headed (in many cases even using an outline), another will eschew plot specifics and outlines altogether. These intrepid word-slingers insist that the story "invent itself" as the work progresses. Hemingway is a prime example of the "let's wait and see" school. Writers like Katherine Anne Porter, in the other camp, insist on knowing exactly how the book will end before they write the first page. Porter writes the last chapter of her novels *first*. Then and only then does she begin Chapter One.

One of the perhaps unexpected pleasures you may derive from *The Quotable Writer* is the book's usefulness in referencing many works that readers will find worthy of further exploration. The "Works Cited" list is a veritable treasure trove of books that harbor not only good reading, but some of the best professional advice and tips on writing you'll find anywhere.

No book can make you a successful writer or good teacher. But books can certainly help. Forgive me if you think I'm going over the top in this observation, but in most enterprises of extraordinary individual effort (and writing certainly qualifies)—before the player takes to the field, the soldier to his mission, the pilot to his plane, or the jockey to his horse, so to speak—a great deal of coaching and pep talk from fellow participants will proceed the event. You may be on your own once the action begins, but, unless you're a fool, the words and experiences of others can help see you through. The voices of other writers, if you will listen to them carefully, can help save you a great deal of aggravation, wasted time, and stumbling down blind alleys to heartbreak.

As an editor and writer of a certain modest success, I frequently hear an inevitable question: "How can I get an agent?" My answer is usually the same: "Not having an agent isn't your problem. Your real problem is that you don't have anything to show a good agent."

And it's true. You've got to pay your dues, and hone the skills of the writing craft. How do you do that? By writing. Writing and eventually selling. Write for your school paper, the op-ed pages of your local newspaper. For trade magazines in your profession or magazines about hobbies and things that interest you. Write, submit, rewrite, and submit some more. Publish! Get paid—something, anything! Develop a professional attitude and respect for your craft and field and the way you handle your work and yourself.

In my own view, talking with other writers and teachers is important. Try workshops, conferences, whatever. If you're young, you'll probably consider moving to New York. You'll be scraping the bottom of the payroll barrel in editorial work, but you'll be among other aspiring writers and editors. Every other person you meet who says he's working on a screenplay or novel will be a phony—wannabes who want to *have written something* but are, in fact, working on nothing at all. These misguided souls just love "talking" the writing game. You'll spot or overhear them at any New York watering hole, often before you even have time to order a drink. But your friends and associates will not be phonies, and your talks with them will be rich with tradecraft and interesting experiences and observations.

There are conflicting views on this subject—conferences, living in New York, contact with other writers. Hemingway advised against all of it in *Green Hills of Africa*, in one of his most infamous pieces of BS, coming as it did after he had spent considerable time living in Paris as a young man surrounded by other writers, editors, and mentors like Ezra Pound. Sorry, Papa, but you fumbled the ball in that quote! (You'll see the quote inside.)

I could go on forever blabbing about writing and writers, subjects I happen to love. But it's about time that I get out of the way. There are many other books you can buy filled with writers' quotes. I hope *The Quotable Writer* will be the one you find the most interesting and useful, whether you're an aspiring writer, a teacher, student, or interested observer.

Lamar Underwood
Spring 2004

1

Words of Wisdom
for
Aspiring Writers

What Works, What Doesn't

The most important advice I would suggest to beginning writers: Try to leave out the parts that readers skip.

ELMORE LEONARD
In *Snoopy's Guide to the Writing Life* (2002)

The best way is to stop when you are going good and when you know what will happen next. If you do that every day when you are writing a novel you will never be stuck. That is the most important thing I can tell you so try to remember it.

ERNEST HEMINGWAY
By-Line: Ernest Hemingway (1967)

A writer should never write about the extraordinary. That is for the journalist.

JAMES JOYCE

One of the few things I know about writing is this: spend it all, shoot it, play it, lose it, all, right away, every time. Do not hoard what seems good . . . give it, give it all, give it now. Something more will arise for later, something better.

ANNIE DILLARD
The Writing Life (1989)

However your world is viewed, it must be your own . . . Only through a vigorous exactitude of presentation can the essential strangeness of life be conveyed . . . You'll never be able to write a novel as long as you have the illusion that . . . the world you know is too dull and commonplace.

JOHN BRAINE
Writing a Novel (1974)

To write well, express yourself like the common people, but think like a wise man.

ARISTOTLE

Many novelists feel that research is an alien word that belongs to writers of fact . . . that they should confine themselves to what they know, or can imagine, and include little else. I disagree with this notion and I am not alone in doing so.

IRVING WALLACE
The Writing of One Novel (1968)

If you are in difficulties with a book, try the element of surprise: attack it at an hour when it isn't expecting it.

H. G. WELLS

Myth: A would-be fiction writer shouldn't read other people's fiction because it will unduly influence his own writing.

Fact: If you don't read other people's fiction, and lots of it, you will never succeed as a writer. Period. There is no other way.

JAMES A. RITCHIE
In *The Writer's Handbook* (1997)

Leave your readers with something experienced, not just something read. Give them an emotional reality. Make it impossible for them simply to chuck your book into the wastebasket when they've finished reading it and grab the next one. Make your novel linger, haunt, last.

T. JEFFERSON PARKER
In *The Writer's Handbook* (1997)

Don't tell me the moon is shining; show me the glint of light on broken glass.

ANTON CHEKHOV

If you write about a bullfighter wetting the edges of his *muleta,* and then stamping it in the sand to give it weight, you do not have to devote a chapter to how hard the wind was blowing that day.

ROBERT RUARK
In *The Lost Classics of Robert Ruark* (1996)

For your writing life to flourish, your mind has to go outwards.

RICHARD FORD
In *Passion and Craft:*
Conversations with Notable Writers (1998)

———————

Reading your work aloud, even silently, is the most astonishingly easy and reliable method that there is for achieving economy in prose, efficiency of description, and narrative effect as well. Rely upon it: if you can read it aloud to yourself without wincing, you have probably gotten it right.

GEORGE V. HIGGINS
On Writing (1990)

You must focus on the writing itself, not . . . rewards. It's like . . . the restaurant with no prices on the menu: If you have to ask the price, you can't afford to eat there. Similarly, if your goal as a writer is anything other than the work itself, you can't afford to be one.

FRED HUNTER
In *The Writer's Handbook* (1997)

—•◦•—

When the amateur writer lets a bad sentence stand in his final draft, . . . the sin is frigidity: He has not yet learned the importance of his art, the only art or science in the world that deals in precise detail with the causes, nature, and effects of extraordinary human feeling.

JOHN GARDNER
The Art of Fiction (1983)

How does one get lost? Through incorrect aims. . . . Through wanting literary fame too quickly. From wanting money too soon. If only we could remember, fame and money are gifts given us only *after* we have gifted the world with our best, our lonely, our individual truths . . .

RAY BRADBURY
Zen in the Art of Writing (1990)

Write without pay until somebody offers you pay. If nobody offers within three years the candidate may look upon the circumstance with the most implicit confidence as the sign that sawing wood is what he was intended for.

MARK TWAIN
In *The Wit and Wisdom of Mark Twain* (1987)

I don't pretend to have all the answers, but I do know this: In order to be a writer you have to write what's in your heart. The moment you try to write about a topic that's currently hot or what you think others believe you ought to do, you're sunk.

ERIC VAN LUSTBADER
In *Writers Write: The Internet Writing Journal* (July 2001)

Take the attitude that what you are thinking and feeling is valuable stuff, and then be naïve enough to get it all down on paper. But be careful: if your intuition says that your story sucks, make sure it really is your intuition and not your mother.

ANNE LAMOTT
Bird by Bird: Some Instructions on Writing and Life (1994)

You would-be Thomas Wolfes and Gertrude Steins out there should understand one thing above all: likely you ain't gonna make no money as a writer. *Real money*, I mean. The kind of money that makes a mother clap hands when her progeny marries you . . .

LARRY L. KING
None but a Blockhead (1986)

Don't listen to doubt. It leads no place but to pain and negativity . . . Instead, have a tenderness and determination toward your writing, a sense of humor and deep patience that you are doing the right thing . . . See beyond [doubt] to the vastness of life and the belief in time and practice.

NATALIE GOLDBERG
Writing Down the Bones (1986)

If I could give one maxim to a young writer, I'd say live with your cowardice. Live with it every day. Hate it or defend it, but don't try to slough it off. Cowardice is a prime cause; literary apathy or writer's block is all too often the effect.

NORMAN MAILER
The Spooky Art (2003)

If reading is your pleasure, *read*, but don't expect the magic to flow from Willa Cather into *you* and the words to come right out of your bone marrow, pre-ordained, and arrange themselves powerfully, perfectly, in sentences and paragraphs. If you want to be a writer, *write*. Write *something*.

HELEN GURLEY BROWN
The Writer's Rules (1998)

I can't count the number of horror stories I hear about the years that are lost, the spirits that are crushed because people choose not to heed the words "You're no good at writing, do something else"—even though they've asked for a frank opinion.

JONI EVANS, PUBLISHING AND ADVERTISING EXECUTIVE
In *The Writer's Rules* (1998) by Helen Gurley Brown

I think that if you want to write, don't write to make money. Write for the fun of it . . . Most beginning authors have no idea of the amount of craft that's involved in putting together a story. They think it will just write itself, that they can just . . . tap it out.

STEPHEN COONTS
In *Writers Write: The Internet Writing Journal* (January 2000)

The most essential gift for a good writer is a built-in, shock-proof shit detector. This is the writer's radar and all great writers have had it.

ERNEST HEMINGWAY
In *Writers at Work, Second Series* (1965)

Writing is self-taught. Consulting other people only teaches you to depend on their reactions, which may or may not be legitimate. Quit looking for approval . . . . Learn to evaluate your own work with a dispassionate eye . . . the lessons you acquire will be all the more valuable because you've mastered your craft from within.

SUE GRAFTON
In *Snoopy's Guide to the Writing Life* (2002)

A budding free-lance writer should live in New York. After all, it's the seat of most magazine offices—and it's where you meet editors by chance. Most commissions have arisen from casual conversations, and contacts are horribly important.

NORA SAYRE
In *Mademoiselle* magazine (March 1968)

Don't burden people on the job with the fascinating news that you are a writer. For one thing they don't give a shit. For another it sounds as though you are trying to be better than they are. You aren't better. Different, not better.

RITA MAE BROWN
Starting from Scratch (1988)

Write about something in which you are a participant. The world needs more books written by writers who are also experts, not writers who are journalists.

DAN POYNTER
In *Getting Your Book Published* (1997)

But the sensibility of the writer, whether fiction or poetry, comes from paying attention. I tell my students that writing doesn't begin when you sit down to write. It's a way of being in the world, and the essence of it is paying attention.

JULIA ALVAREZ
In *Passion and Craft:
Conversations with Notable Writers* (1998)

Writers should work alone. They should see each other only after their work is done, and not too often then. Otherwise they become like writers in New York. All angleworms in a bottle, trying to derive knowledge and nourishment from their own contact and from the bottle.

ERNEST HEMINGWAY
Green Hills of Africa (1935)

———

It is necessary to remember at all times, especially when most frustrated and cranky, that *the writer is always at the mercy of his story.* Some stories are better than others. There isn't anything that the writer can do to change this.

GEORGE V. HIGGINS
On Writing (1990)

Advice to young writers who want to get ahead without any annoying delays: don't write about Man, write about *a* man.

E. B. WHITE

You can approach the act of writing with nervousness, excitement, hopefulness, or even despair . . . You can come to the act with your fists clenched and your eyes narrowed, ready to kick ass and take down names . . . Come to it any way but lightly . . . *you must not come lightly to the blank page.*

STEPHEN KING
On Writing (2000)

Don't beat about the bush—go straight to the point. Avoid analogies of the "just as, so too" variety. Avoid superlatives, generalizations, and platitudes. Be specific and factual. Be enthusiastic, friendly, and memorable. Don't be a bore. Tell the truth, but make the truth fascinating.

DAVID OGILVY
Confessions of an Advertising Man (1963)

The danger of planning to do several drafts lies in the subconscious or unconscious attitude that, *If I don't get it right this time, it's okay; I can work it out in a later draft.* This encourages carelessness . . . The more things you write with this approach in mind, the sloppier you become . . .

DEAN R. KOONTZ
Writing Popular Fiction (1972)

Relevance—the question of it—is the headache of novel-writing . . . The most striking fault in work by young or beginning novelists submitted for criticism, is irrelevance—due either to infatuation or indecision.

> ELIZABETH BOWEN
> *Collected Impressions* (1950)

Breslin's Rule: Don't trust a brilliant idea unless it survives a hangover.

> JIMMY BRESLIN

6. Thou shall infect thy reader with anxiety, stress, and tension, for those conditions that he deplores in life he relishes in fiction.

> SOL STEIN
> *Stein on Writing* (1995),
> from "Ten Commandments for Writers"

The opening's not everything. You can start off with *Call me Ishmael* and still lose your reader down the line if you're not careful. But your opening *has* to be good—or the rest of the story won't have a chance because nobody'll stick around to read it.

> LAWRENCE BLOCK
> *Telling Lies for Fun and Profit* (1981)

But your chances with a first novel are the greatest . . . Your voice is a new voice, there has been none like it before. Your story is new because you've never told a story before . . . Your first novel isn't your only chance of success, but it is your best chance.

> JOHN BRAINE
> *Writing a Novel* (1974)

The most important sentence in any article is the first one. If it doesn't induce the reader to proceed to the second sentence . . . I urge you not to count on the reader to stick around. He is a fidgety fellow who wants to know—very soon—what's in it for him.

WILLIAM ZINSSER
On Writing Well: An Informal Guide to Writing Nonfiction (1985)

I once asked Sinclair Lewis how best to handle flashbacks. "Don't," was his complete reply.

BARNABY CONRAD
The Complete Guide to Writing Fiction (1990)

Begin in the middle of a scene or event. Keep pushing forward rather than stopping to inform the reader of background details. Known as *beginning in medias res,* in the middle of things, this opening supplies a quick start to your story.

JACK HEFFRON
The Writer's Idea Book (2000)

In writing love scenes, especially, trust your reader's imagination. I've written my share of extremely explicit scenes, but I believe my most memorable ones were those in which I focused on what my characters were feeling and thinking, rather than on what they were doing.

JOAN DIAL
In *Good Advice on Writing* (1992)

Cut out all those exclamation marks. An exclamation mark is like laughing at your own joke.

F. SCOTT FITZGERALD
In *Beloved Infidel* (1959)

Even the slightest thing contains a little that is unknown. We must find it. To describe a blazing fire or a tree in a plain, we must remain before that fire or tree until they no longer resemble for us any other tree or any other fire.

That is the way to become original.

> GUSTAVE FLAUBERT, ADVICE TO GUY DE MAUPASSANT
> Recalled by de Maupassant in Preface, *Pierre et Jean* (1888)

Beware the word *there,* deadener of prose.

There was something that smelled bad. Something smelled bad.

> OAKLEY HALL
> *The Art and Craft of Novel Writing* (1989)

I repeat: *the things that wear you down are also the things that nurture your talent.*

PHILIP ROTH
The Facts (1988)

There's a trick I'm going to share with you. I learned it almost twenty years ago and I've never forgotten it. . . . So pay attention.

Don't begin at the beginning.

LAWRENCE BLOCK
Writing the Novel: From Plot to Print (1979)

You have to learn how to read your work; I don't mean enjoy it because you wrote it. I mean . . . read it as though it is the first time you've ever seen it. Critique it that way. Don't get all involved in your thrilling sentences and all that . . .

TONI MORRISON
In *Women Writers at Work: The Paris Review Interviews* (1998)

Remember: what lasts in the reader's mind is not the phrase but the effect the phrase created: laughter, tears, pain, joy. If the phrase is not affecting the reader, what is it *doing* there? Make it do its job or cut it without mercy or remorse.

ISAAC ASIMOV
How to Enjoy Writing (1987)

You know, it's not exactly a natural pursuit, a man putting himself in front of a typewriter—a machine—day after day. But you've got to spend three or four years digging yourself a rut so deep that finally you find it more convenient not to get out of it.

ERNEST HAYCOX
In *Ernest Haycox* (1996)

Wannabes, dreamers, enrollees in creative writing workshops, attendees at writers' conferences, sidewalk pounders and country walkers indulging your fantasies of fame and fortune! It takes *years* for us to understand what we can accomplish and where our work can take us. And you can't reach it in a single book.

SUZANNE LIPSETT
Surviving a Writer's Life (1994)

Kaplan's Law of Words: Any words that aren't working for you are working against you. So weed them out. If a word—yes, any single word—isn't adding something we don't know *and need to know*, it's adding nothing. Worse, it's distracting. It's slowing down the prose.

DAVID MICHAEL KAPLAN
Revision: A Creative Approach to Writing and Rewriting Fiction (1997)

Young scholars generally wish to secure the last fact before writing anything, like General McClellan refusing to advance (as people said) until the last mule was shod . . . Half the pleas I have heard from graduate students for more time or another grant-in-aid are mere excuses to postpone the painful drudgery of writing.

SAMUEL ELIOT MORISON
In *Sailor Historian: The Best of Samuel Eliot Morison* (1977)

Boozing does not necessarily have to go hand in hand with being a writer, as seems to be the concept in America. I therefore solemnly declare to all young men trying to become writers that they do not actually have to become drunkards first.

JAMES JONES
In *Writers at Work: The Paris Review Interviews, Third Series* (1967)

How vain it is to sit down to write when you have not stood up to live.

HENRY DAVID THOREAU

Less is found in what are ungraciously called "slush piles" today because fewer editors fish in such waters, and many book and magazine publishers even flatly refuse to accept unsolicited manuscripts because the odds are so poor, the dross so thick.

NICK LYONS
"No, No, a Thousand Times No", in *The New York Times Book Review* (July 26, 1992)

I have edited and published both kinds of writers and both kinds of books [literary and commercial, fiction and nonfiction]. I have worked closely with writers of each kind who have made millions from a single work. What I have never witnessed is a writer's work succeeding notably in a field he doesn't habitually read for pleasure.

SOL STEIN
Stein on Writing (1995)

The type of thing which is practically impossible for the beginner to conceive, execute and sell, is the writing with a "Message!" About half the potential five million writers usually current get knocked off by this stumbling block . . . *"Books with messages don't sell well unless the messenger is tremendously well known."*

JACK WOODFORD
Writer's Cramp (1953)

The worst mistakes? [In manuscripts by first-time authors.] I think writing a story that they perceive as saleable that they're not truly invested in. "Legal thrillers are selling; I should write a legal thriller. I have some law experience." . . . And it doesn't work. It just doesn't work.

JENNIFER SAWYER FISHER, SENIOR EDITOR, AVON BOOKS
In *Writers Write: The Internet Writing Journal* (April 1999)

You hear a lot about slanting for the commercial markets, but not enough about slanting for the literary cliques. Both approaches, in the final analysis, are unhappy ways for a writer to live in this world.

RAY BRADBURY
Zen in the Art of Writing (1990)

Darlene [Geiss] told her husband that *Valley* made her feel "as if I'd picked up the telephone and was listening to two women telling how their husbands are in bed. You can't hang up on a conversation like that. And once the book is edited and straightened out, you can't stop reading it."

BARBARA SEAMAN

Lovely Me, The Life of Jacqueline Susann (1987)

[AFTER CONSIDERABLE EDITORIAL "REPAIRS" BY EDITORS AND JACQUELINE SUSANN HERSELF, *Valley of the Dolls*, PUBLISHED BY BERNARD GEISS ASSOCIATES, WENT ON TO BECOME ONE OF THE BIGGEST BEST SELLERS IN HISTORY.]

Last year four of my students sold novels . . . Why them and not the one-hundred-forty-six other students? Simple. *They finished their books* . . . The true test of whether you're a real novelist isn't that you're working on a book. It's that you finished one.

RAYMOND OBSTFELD
In *The Writer's Digest Handbook of Novel Writing* (1992)

Publishing a volume of poetry is like dropping a rose petal down the Grand Canyon and waiting for the echo.

DON MARQUIS
Sun Dial Time (1936)

A good many young writers make the mistake of enclosing a stamped, self-addressed envelope, big enough for the manuscript to come back in. This is too much of a temptation to the editor.

RING LARDNER
Preface, *How to Write Short Stories* (1924)

To publish a work of novel length, one must find . . . some means of satisfying the ordinary reader's first requirement for any piece of writing longer than fifteen pages, namely profluence—the sense that things are moving, getting somewhere, flowing forward. The common reader demands some reason to keep turning the pages.

JOHN GARDNER
On Becoming a Novelist (1983)

I can remember having several shoe boxes filled with rejection notices—thousands of those antiseptic slips, most uncontaminated by human word. How I leaped when I finally received a first "Try us again" or a "Not bad" or a scrawled "Not quite for us but thanks."

NICK LYONS
"No, No, a Thousand Times No", in *The New York Times Book Review* (July 26, 1992)

2

The Student Writer: Courses and Workshops

Lessons in Futility or Truly Beneficial?

Everywhere I go I'm asked if I think the universities stifle writers. My opinion is that they don't stifle enough of them. There's many a best-seller that could have been prevented by a good teacher.

FLANNERY O'CONNOR
In *The Writer's Craft* (1974)

The answer is that you can't find no school in operation up to date, whether it be a general institution of learning or a school that specializes in story writing, which can make a great author out of a born druggist.

RING LARDNER
Preface, *How to Write Short Stories* (1924)

Writing students advised to "write what ya know about" may feel restricted to parochial settings . . . Stephen Crane had never been near a war when he wrote *The Red Badge of Courage.* The task is not to know a subject firsthand, but to be a step ahead of the readers . . .

ARTHUR PLOTNIK
Honk if You're a Writer (1992)

Our managing editor [at *Cosmopolitan* magazine], Guy Flatley, always said you couldn't denigrate what anybody learned in college or from *writing* in college. The more writing the better . . .

HELEN GURLEY BROWN
The Writer's Rules (1998)

When I used to teach creative writing, I would tell my students to make their characters want something right away. . . . When you exclude plot, when you exclude anybody's wanting anything, you exclude the reader . . .

KURT VONNEGUT JR.
In *Writers at Work: Sixth Series* (1984)

The young writer that is . . . demon-driven and wants to learn . . . he will learn from almost any source that he finds. He will learn from other people who are not writers, he will learn from writers, but he learns it— you can't teach it.

WILLIAM FAULKNER
In *Faulkner in the University: Class Conferences at the University of Virginia* (1957–58)

At one school . . . in New York . . . there are a couple of teachers who moon in the most disgusting way over the poorest, most talentless writers, giving false hope where there shouldn't be any hope at all. Regularly they put out dreary little anthologies, the quality of which would chill your blood.

WILLIAM STYRON
In *Writers at Work: The Paris Review Interviews* (1958)

Any way you can associate with writers is bound to be to your advantage. Taking a writing course will put you in touch with at least one published author, the teacher (there may be others among the students). Ask instructors for the names of people you should send your work to . . .

JUDITH APPELBAUM
How to Get Happily Published, Third Edition (1988)

I know that the student longs for help, but what he develops in a writing course is generally a psychological dependency. He asks the teacher . . . to support him against an incredulous world which will not allow him to take things into his own hands and declare himself a writer.

SAUL BELLOW
In *The Contemporary Writer* (1972)

It takes as long to learn writing skills as it does to become a neurosurgeon. This society constructed an apprentice system for the neurosurgeon. It has built nothing for the writer. . . . One alternative chosen by many writers is journalism. This is a much better choice than hanging around the university.

RITA MAE BROWN
Starting from Scratch (1988)

In the past few years I've assigned books to be read before a student attends one of my weeklong seminars. I have been astonished by how few people—people who supposedly want to write—read books, and if they read them, how little they examine them.

NATALIE GOLDBERG
Thunder and Lightning: Cracking Open the Writer's Craft (2000)

In fact, the most of the successful authors of the short fiction of today never went to no kind of a college, or if they did, they studied piano tuning or the barber trade.

RING LARDNER
Preface, *How to Write Short Stories* (1924)

———•••———

Writing teachers invariably tell students: Write about what you know. That's, of course, what you have to do, but on the other hand, how do you know what you know until you've written about it. Writing is knowing. What did Kafka know? The insurance business?

E. L. DOCTOROW
In *Writers at Work: The Paris Review Interviews, Eighth Series* (1988)

The old saw "Write about what you know" can produce deadly stuff when the author isn't old enough to vote or buy a beer; word exercises are just that, and creative writing assignments tend to read like creative writing assignments.

RICHARD PRICE
"Writers on Writing", *The New York Times* (January 13, 2002)

I don't know much about creative writing programs. But they're not telling the truth if they don't teach, one, that writing is hard work, and, two, that you have to give up a great deal of life, your personal life, to be a writer.

DORIS LESSING

The idea of being a writer attracts a good many shiftless people, those who are merely burdened with poetic feelings or afflicted with sensibility.

FLANNERY O'CONNOR
In *Mystery and Manners* (1969)

3

The Writer's Craft: How the Pros Master It

Discipline
Ideas and Inspiration
Style
Language
Viewpoint
Characterization
The Short Story
Work Habits

Discipline

Get to the desk regularly. The writers we admire . . . might be geniuses whose talents dwarf ours, but more they're people who show up. . . . If you want to write, you must begin by beginning, continue by continuing, finish by finishing. This is the great secret. . . . Tell no one.

JACK HEFFRON
The Writer's Idea Book (2000)

True ease in writing comes from art, not chance,
As those move easiest who have learn'd to dance.

ALEXANDER POPE
An Essay on Criticism (1711)

All writers know that on some golden mornings they are touched by the wand—are on intimate terms with poetry and cosmic truth. I have experienced these moments myself. Their lesson is simple: It's a total illusion. And the danger in the illusion is that you will wait for those moments.

JOHN KENNETH GALBRAITH

Planning to write is not writing. Outlining . . . researching . . . talking to people about what you're doing, none of that is writing. Writing is writing.

E. L. DOCTOROW

The best way is to read it [a novel in progress] all every day from the start, correcting as you go along . . . When it gets so long . . . read back two or three chapters each day; then each week read it all from the start. That's how to make it all of one piece.

ERNEST HEMINGWAY
By-Line: Ernest Hemingway (1967)

Writing is about hypnotizing yourself into believing in yourself, getting some work done, then unhypnotizing yourself and going over the material coldly. There will be many mistakes, many things to take out and others that need to be added. You just aren't always going to make the right decision.

ANNE LAMOTT
Bird by Bird: Some Instructions on Writing and Life (1994)

I hear people say they're going to write. I ask, when? They give me vague statements. Indefinite plans get dubious results. When we're concrete about our writing time, it alleviates that thin constant feeling of anxiety that writers have . . .

NATALIE GOLDBERG
Thunder and Lightning: Cracking Open the Writer's Craft (2000)

Writing is play in the same way that playing the piano is "play," or putting on a theatrical "play" is play. Just because something's fun doesn't mean it isn't serious.

MARGARET ATWOOD

I have never thought writing novels was hard work. Hard work was commercial fishing out of New Bedford . . . Novels have more to do with desire—translating desire into prose—and a temperament that accepts concentration over the long haul, meaning the ability to sit alone in one place day by day.

WARD JUST
In *Writers on Writing: Collected Essays from* The New York Times (2001)

The art of writing, like the art of love, runs all the way from a kind of routine hard to distinguish from piling bricks to a kind of frenzy closely related to *delirium tremens.*

H. L. MENCKEN
Minority Report (1956)

You write by sitting down and writing . . . How one works, assuming he's disciplined, doesn't matter. If he or she is not disciplined, no sympathetic magic will help . . . everyone learns his or her own best way. The real mystery to crack is *you.*

BERNARD MALAMUD
In *Writers at Work, Sixth Series* (1984)

Many times I just sit for three hours with no ideas coming to me. But I know one thing: if an idea does come between nine and twelve, I am there ready for it.

FLANNERY O'CONNOR
In *How to Get Happily Published,* Third Edition (1988)

You can sit there, tense and worried, freezing the creative energies, or you can start writing *something,* perhaps something silly. It simply doesn't matter *what* . . . In five or ten minutes the imagination will heat, the tightness will fade, and a certain spirit and rhythm will take over.

LEONARD S. BERNSTEIN
Getting Published: The Writer in the Combat Zone (1986)

Once you are into the novel it is cowardly to worry about whether you can go on the next day. . . . You have to go on. So there is no sense to worry. You have to learn that to write a novel. The hard part about a novel is to finish it.

ERNEST HEMINGWAY
By-Line: Ernest Hemingway (1967)

Ideas and Inspiration

You don't write because you want to say something, you write because you've got something to say.

> F. SCOTT FITZGERALD
> *The Crack-Up* (1945)

Books choose their authors; the act of creation is not entirely a rational and conscious one.

> SALMAN RUSHDIE
> In *The Independent* (February 4, 1990)

If a writer is honest, if what is at stake for him can seem to matter to his readers, then his work may be read. But a writer will work anyway, as I do, as I have, in part to explore this *terra incognita*, this dangerous ground I seem to need to risk.

FREDERICK BUSCH
A Dangerous Profession (1998)

We write to taste life twice, in the moment, and in retrospection. . . . We write to be able to transcend our life, to reach beyond it. We write to teach ourselves to speak with others, to record the journey into the labyrinth.

ANAÏS NIN

I had a large vocabulary and had been reading constantly since childhood. I had taken words and the art of arranging them.

MAYA ANGELOU

—•••—

To evoke in oneself a feeling one has once experienced and having evoked it in oneself by means of movements, lines, colors, sounds, or forms expressed in words, so to transmit that feeling—this is the activity of art.

LEO TOLSTOY
What Is Art? (1898)

When talented people write badly, it's generally for one of two reasons: Either they're blinded by an idea they feel compelled to prove or they're driven by an emotion they must express. When talented people work well, it is generally for this reason: They're moved by a desire to touch the audience.

ROBERT MCKEE
Story (1997)

The thing that most frustrates me in being around arriving writers of whatever age is my inability or anyone else's inability to make them understand how those wonderful things are always there . . . these undisclosed treasures . . . locked in their lives . . . It's there. It's not on the Siberian frontier.

THOMAS McGUANE
In *The Complete Guide to Writing Fiction* (1990)

Our ideas and intentions can mask and cover up a story; there is a life force that will declare itself if you let it. Get out of the way.

NATALIE GOLDBERG

Thunder and Lightning: Cracking Open the Writer's Craft (2000)

I began to see what my material might be: the city street from whose mixed life we had held aloof, and the country life before that, with the ways and manners of remembered India. . . . Almost at the same time came the language, the tone, the voice for that material.

V. S. NAIPAUL
Reading and Writing: A Personal Account (2000)

What do you think of the world? You, the prism, measure the light of the world; it burns through your mind to throw a different spectroscopic reading onto white paper than anyone else anywhere can throw.

RAY BRADBURY
Zen in the Art of Writing (1990)

Show me a hero and I will write you a tragedy.

F. SCOTT FITZGERALD
The Crack-Up (1936)

———

But the author does not only write when he is at his desk; he writes all day long, when he is thinking, when he is reading, when he is experiencing; everything he sees and feels is significant to his purpose and, consciously or unconsciously, he is . . . storing and making over his impressions.

W. SOMERSET MAUGHAM
The Summing Up (1938)

No, it [an actual real-life incident recalled in a play] is not autobiographical. An incident happens to you and it gives your imagination a starting point. But you turn it into someone else's experience, hoping that it touches a nerve of identification in other people . . .

NEIL SIMON
Rewrites (1996)

I never drink while I'm working, but after a few glasses, I get ideas that would never have occurred to me dead sober. And some of the ideas turn out to be valuable the next day. Some not.

IRWIN SHAW
In *Writers at Work, Fifth Series* (1981)

I can never forsake the work that got me where I am—the dogged research into time of death, the slide in the lab, the slab in the morgue. . . . If I stop seeing, hearing, touching, there will be no story. I will be a writer with nothing to say . . .

PATRICIA CORNWELL
In *The Writing Life:*
Collection from Washington Post Book World (2003)

I wanted [to write a novel] . . . so much that I came to think of myself as being a novelist even though I had never written one. . . . I was a free-lance magazine writer then, . . . and I saw myself as a victim of the literary sharecropper system . . .

ROBERT CRICHTON
In *Afterwords: Novelists on Their Novels* (1969)

If you're a writer, the assimilation of important experiences almost obliges you to write about them. Writing is how you make the experience your own, how you explore what it means to you, how you come to possess it, and ultimately release it.

MICHAEL CRICHTON
Travels (1988)

The advantage, the luxury, as well as the torment and responsibility of the novelist, is that there is no limit to what he many attempt as an executant—no limit to his possible experiments, efforts, discoveries, successes.

HENRY JAMES
The Art of Fiction (1888)

I learned . . . that inspiration does not come like a bolt, nor is it kinetic, energetic striving, but it comes into us slowly and quietly and all the time, though we must regularly and every day give it a little chance to start flowing, prime it with a little solitude and idleness.

BRENDA UELAND

[To write a novel] you need . . . a strong central image that yields a strong situation, or series of situations. By strong, I don't necessarily mean strongly dramatic. I mean strong in the sense of tenacious, one that won't let you off the hook.

PAUL SCOTT
On Writing and the Novel (1987)

The standards we raise [as individual readers] and the judgments we pass steal into the air, and become part of the atmosphere which writers breathe as they work. An influence is created which tells upon them even if it never finds its way into print.

VIRGINIA WOOLF
The Second Common Reader (1932)

I will maintain that the artist needs only this: a special world of which he alone has the key.

ANDRÉ GIDE
In *Woman Writer: Occasions and Opportunities* (1988)

There is no such thing as a holy experience for writers. You don't have to go on the rodeo circuit or fight bulls, or go to war. You just have to write well and truly understand what your subject is. . . . When you touch it right everybody gets it.

THOMAS MCGUANE
In *The Complete Guide to Writing Fiction* (1990)

In the beginning there's something very nebulous, a state of alert, a wariness, a curiosity. Something I perceive in the fog and vagueness which arouses my interest, curiosity, and excitement and then translates itself into work, note cards, the summary of the plot.

MARIO VARGAS LLOSA
In *The Paris Review* (Issue 116, 1990)

Memory is the diary that we all carry with us.

OSCAR WILDE
The Importance of Being Earnest (1893)

I was lying in bed . . . when suddenly this line [the first line of *Catch-22*] came to me: "It was love at first sight. The first time he saw the chaplain, *Someone* fell madly in love with him." I didn't have the name Yossarian . . . the book began to evolve clearly in my mind . . .

JOSEPH HELLER
The Writer's Chapbook: The Paris Review Interviews (1989)

The search for a story is a matter of slowly, calmly, carefully, tentatively coaxing a hidden set of some-things into visibility: Those somethings may be char-acters, places, situations, scenes, hopes, fears—the unseen possibilities of drama that are lurking in what we know.

STEPHEN KOCH
The Modern Library Writer's Workshop:
A Guide to the Craft of Fiction (2003)

"The cat sat on the mat" is not the beginning of a story. "The cat sat on the dog's mat" is.

JOHN LE CARRE
In *The Modern Library Writer's Workshop* (2003)

A play just seems to materialize, like an apparition; it gets clearer and clearer and clearer. It's very vague at first, as in the case of *Streetcar* . . . I simply had the vision of a woman in her late youth . . . she'd been stood up by the man she planned to marry.

TENNESSEE WILLIAMS
In *Writers at Work, Sixth Series* (1984)

Style

The greatest thing in style is to have command of metaphor.

ARISTOTLE

———

The "key" to most works of fiction is a voice, a rhythm, a unique music; a precise way of *seeing* and *hearing* that will give the writer access to the world he is trying to create . . .

JOYCE CAROL OATES
Woman Writer: Occasions and Opportunities (1988)

Style and Structure are the essence of a book; great ideas are hogwash.

VLADIMIR NABOKOV
In *Writers at Work, Fourth Series* (1976)

———

In fiction what counts is not expertise at all, but the illusion of expertise . . . With enough accurate detail to stay ahead of the reader, the fiction writer can tackle any subject . . . Some genres have certain conventions that need attention, but the rest is energy, imagination, and a way with words.

ARTHUR PLOTNIK
Honk if You're a Writer (1992)

Writing free verse is like playing tennis with the net down.

ROBERT FROST
Address at Milton Academy, Milton, Massachusetts (1935)

————

If he were a writer, when he tried to write, out of some particular day, he found in the effort that he could recall exactly how the light fell and how the temperature felt, and all the quality of it . . . that ability is at the bottom of writing, I am sure.

MAXWELL PERKINS
In *Max Perkins: Editor of Genius* (1978)
[IN A LETTER TO ASPIRING NOVELIST JAMES JONES, 1946, WHEN JONES WAS BEGINNING HIS WORK ON *From Here to Eternity*.]

What then will the style [of *East of Eden*] be? I don't know. Books establish their own pace. This I have found out. As soon as the story starts its style will establish itself.

JOHN STEINBECK
Journal of a Novel: The East of Eden *Letters* (1969)

⸻

The art of fiction does not begin until the novelist thinks of his story as a matter to be *shown*, to be so exhibited that it will tell itself.

PERCY LUBBOCK
The Craft of Fiction (1921)

Style . . . is all rhythm . . . A sight, an emotion, creates this wave in the mind, long before it makes words to fit it; and in writing . . . one has to recapture this, and set this working . . . and then, as it breaks and rumbles in the mind, it makes words to fit in.

VIRGINIA WOOLF
Letter to Vita Sackville-West (1928)

The best description of style I have ever read and one of the most valuable lines about writing is by . . . [Denis Donoghue] . . . who says: Style is the right feeling animating the *voice*.

ROBERT CRICHTON
In *Afterwords: Novelists on Their Novels* (1969)

Style is as much under the words as in the words.

GUSTAVE FLAUBERT
Letter to Ernest Freydeau (1860)

An author arrives at a good style when his language performs what is required of it without shyness.

CYRIL CONNOLLY
Enemies of Promise (1938)

What can we writers learn from lizards, lift from birds? In quickness is truth. The faster you blurt . . . the more honest you are. In hesitation is thought. In delay comes the effort for a style, instead of leaping upon truth which is the *only* style worth deadfalling or tiger-trapping.

RAY BRADBURY
Zen in the Art of Writing (1990)

Unfortunately, there is no royal road to style. It cannot be attained by mere industry; it can never be attained through imitation . . . We can still read Macaulay with admiration and pleasure . . . but anyone who tried to imitate Macaulay today would be a pompous ass.

SAMUEL ELIOT MORISON
In *Sailor Historian: The Best of Samuel Eliot Morison* (1977)

Excitement is simple: excitement is a situation, a single event. It mustn't be wrapped up in thoughts, similes, metaphors. A simile is a form of reflection, but excitement is of the moment when there is no time to reflect.

GRAHAM GREENE
A Sort of Life (1971)

I don't think it [style] can be taught. Style results more from what a person is than from what he knows. But there are a few hints that can be thrown out to advantage . . . They would be the twenty-one hints I threw out in Chapter V of *The Elements of Style* [written with William Strunk Jr.].

E. B. White

In *Writers at Work: The Paris Review Interviews, Eighth Series* (1988)

A writer who describes visible objects falsely and violates the propriety of characters, a writer who makes the mountains "nod their drowsy heads" at night . . . violates the first great law of his art. His imitation is altogether unlike the thing imitated.

Thomas Babington Macaulay

Macaulay: Prose and Poetry (1952)

I am of the opinion that the reader each writer wants is part and parcel of the novel's conception. His special presence is evoked in the style and texture of each line. What we call style is the explicit inclusion of some readers in, and all other readers out.

WRIGHT MORRIS
In *Afterwords: Novelists on Their Novels* (1969)

———

I want the reader to turn the page and keep on turning to the end. This is accomplished only when the narrative moves steadily ahead, not when it comes to a weary standstill, overloaded with every item uncovered in the research.

BARBARA TUCHMAN
In *Good Advice on Writing* (1992)

Language

The difference between the *almost*-right word and the *right* word is really a large matter—it's the difference between the lightning bug and the lightning.

Mark Twain
Letter to George Bainton (1888)

It's not what you said that counts; it's what they heard.

J. WALTER THOMPSON AGENCY, NEW YORK, ATTRIBUTED
Copywriter Dictum

———•✦•———

The human language is like a cracked kettle on which we beat out tunes for bears to dance to, when all the time we are longing to move the stars to pity.

GUSTAVE FLAUBERT
Madame Bovary (1857)

———•✦•———

What I like in a good author is not what he says, but what he whispers.

LOGAN PEARSALL SMITH
In *Good Advice on Writing* (1992)

But I discovered when I was very young . . . that nothing could so quickly cast doubt on, and even destroy, an author's characters as bad dialog [O'Hara's spelling]. If people did not talk right, they were not real people. The closer to real talk, the closer to real people . . .

> JOHN O'HARA
> In *John O'Hara on Writers and Writing* (1977)

This is the sort of English up with which I will not put.

> WINSTON CHURCHILL
> [HIS REMARK ON AVOIDING PREPOSITIONS AT THE END OF A SENTENCE.]

It is possible to overuse the well-turned fragment . . . but frags can also work beautifully to streamline narration, create clear images, and create tension as well as to vary the prose-line. A series of grammatically proper sentences can stiffen that line, make it less pliable.

Stephen King
On Writing (2000)

If a writer of prose knows enough about what he is writing about he may omit things that he knows and the reader, if the writer is writing truly enough, will have a feeling of those things as strongly as though the writer had stated them.

Ernest Hemingway
Death in the Afternoon (1932)

Poetry should surprise by a fine excess, and not by singularity. It should strike the reader as a wording of his own highest thoughts, and appear almost as a remembrance.

JOHN KEATS
Letter to John Taylor (1818)

———

Phonetic spelling may be the easiest way to indicate dialect peculiarities, but it is a crude device. Misspelled words tend to jump off the page and assume undue importance, and the apostrophes indicating missed letters take on the appearance of barbed-wire entanglements.

OAKLEY HALL
The Art and Craft of Novel Writing (1989)

Viewpoint

The futility of all prefaces I long ago realized; for the more a writer strives to make his views clear, the more confusion he creates.

JOHANN WOLFGANG VON GOETHE
Poetry and Truth (1749–1832)

———•••———

War talk by men who have been in a war is always interesting, whereas moon talk by a poet who has not been in the moon is likely to be dull.

MARK TWAIN
Life on the Mississippi (1883)

The shifts in point of view can enrich a story, give it depth, give it subtlety, make it mysterious, ambiguous, multifaceted; or they can smother and crush it if instead of causing events to multiply of their own accord. . . . [T]hese displays of technique . . . give rise to incongruities and gratuitous complications . . .

MARIO VARGAS LLOSA
Letters to a Young Novelist (1997)

It's akin to style . . . but it isn't style alone. It is the writer's particular and unmistakable signature on everything he writes. It is his world and no other . . . a writer who has some special way of looking at things and who gives artistic expression to that way of looking.

RAYMOND CARVER
Fires: Essays, Poems, Stories (1985)

No amount of editing and polishing will have any appreciable effect on the flavour of how a man writes. It is the product of the quality of his emotion and perception; it is the ability to transfer these to paper which makes him a writer . . .

RAYMOND CHANDLER
In *Raymond Chandler Speaking* (1977)

The chief difference between good writing and better writing may be measured by the number of imperceptible hesitations the reader experiences as he goes along. The author functions as a kind of forest guide. Does our reader trip over unfamiliar words . . . stub his toe on an ambiguous antecedent?

JAMES J. KILPATRICK
The Writer's Art (1984)

Characterization

The great man is too often all of a piece; it is the little man that is a bundle of contradictory elements. He is inexhaustible. You never come to the end of the surprises he has in store for you.

> W. Somerset Maugham
> *The Summing Up* (1938)

The viewpoint character should be the person with everything at risk, to maintain reader interest and involvement . . . Viewpoint characters, to be interesting, must be *active!*

> Jack M. Bickham
> *Writing and Selling Your Novel* (1996)

I do not know if Freud made the difference, or the very grave and very colorless events of the century itself; but at some point, the people in novels stopped galloping all over the countryside and started brooding from chairs. Everything became psychological and interiorized. External conflict became internal tension.

ANNIE DILLARD
Living in Fiction (1982)

The people in a novel are people the author is going to live with for two years or more. He is going to sleep with them, love them, hate them, betray and perhaps even murder them, and he must be comfortable with the names he gives them.

JOHN GREGORY DUNNE
Harp (1989)

The speciality of the novel is that the writer can talk about his characters as well as through them or can arrange for us to listen when they talk to themselves. He has access to self-communings, and from that level he can descend even deeper and peer into the subconscious.

E. M. FORSTER
Aspects of the Novel (1927)

I want to put a group of characters (perhaps a pair, perhaps even just one) in some sort of predicament and then watch them try to work themselves free. . . . The situation comes first. The characters—always flat and unfeatured to begin with—come next.

STEPHEN KING
On Writing (2000)

The protagonist is *the character whose fate matters most to the story.* And that, in turn, is the character whose fate matters most to you.

STEPHEN KOCH
*The Modern Library Writer's Workshop:
A Guide to the Craft of Fiction* (2003)

"There's no play without characters. First you get your characters, then you get the story, then you get the dialogue. If you got a story and dialogue but no characters, what have you got?"

[Neil Simon answers]: "A sand castle."

[PRODUCER SAM GORDON AFTER TELLING NEIL SIMON THAT AN EARLY DRAFT OF SIMON'S FIRST PLAY, *Come Blow Your Horn*, HAD GOOD DIALOGUE BUT WAS LIKE "A HOUSE BUILT ON SAND." SIMON TOOK GORDON'S ADVICE TO HEART AND ADOPTED IT AS A VIRTUAL MANTRA FOR HIS WORK.]

NEIL SIMON
Rewrites (1996)

. . . I'm letting the people [characters] write their own story themselves. For example, I had written three hundred pages of *Eternity* [*From Here to Eternity*] before I realized that Warden was going to have an affair with Karen Holmes. So I had to go back and bring that about.

JAMES JONES
In *Writers at Work:*
The Paris Review Interviews, Third Series (1967)

I paraphrase Aristotle: . . . to be comical, write about people to whom the audience can feel superior; if you want to be tragical, write about at least one person to whom the audience is bound to feel inferior; and no fair having human problems solved by dumb luck or heavenly intervention.

KURT VONNEGUT JR.
In *Writers on Writing:*
Collected Essays from The New York Times (2001)

Exaggeration is the first step toward creating vivid fictional characters. . . . Time after time I have been confronted by new writers whose novels were peopled with characters who were flat, dull, unclear, uninspiring, uninteresting and plain old boring. . . . *Good characters are not real people; they are better than real people.*

JACK M. BICKHAM
Writing and Selling Your Novel (1996)

Characters take on life sometimes by luck, but I suspect it is when you can write most entirely out of yourself, inside the skin, heart, mind, and soul of a person who is not yourself, that a character becomes in his own right another human being on the page.

EUDORA WELTY
One Writer's Beginnings (1983)

The Short Story

Although the short story is said to have lost its popularity, this is not my experience; thousands of addicts still delight in it because it is above all memorable and is not simply read, but re-read . . . It is the glancing form of fiction . . . right for the nervousness and restlessness of contemporary life.

V. S. PRITCHETT
Preface, *Collected Stories* (1982)

A short story is not as restrictive as a sonnet, but, of all the literary forms, it is possibly the most single-minded. Its aim, as it was identified by . . . Edgar Allan Poe, is to create "an effect" . . . something almost physical, like a sensation. . . . Every word in a story, Poe said, is in the service of that effect.

Louis Menand
In *The New Yorker* (December 1, 2003)

The short story is a difficult literary form, demanding more attention in control and balance than the novel. It is the choice of most beginning writers, attracted to its brevity, its apparent friendliness (a deception) to slender themes, or even its perceived function as a testing ground before attempting the five-hundred-page novel.

E. ANNIE PROULX
Introduction, *Best American Short Stories 1997*

Too often the contemporary short story is about someone ambivalent, ruminative and passive: exactly the sort of character who could never carry a novel (and a personality type common among writers themselves) . . . they stumble haplessly through the motions of the Crumbling Marriage story and the Dying Relative story . . .

SUE MILLER
"Long Story Short", in *The New York Times Book Review* (November 2, 2003)

I love the intricacy of the short form, the speed with which it can change from scene to scene. I have always thought that the writer of short stories is a mixture of reporter, aphoristic wit, moralist and poet—though not "poetical"; he is something of a ballad maker . . .

V. S. PRITCHETT
Preface, *Collected Stories* (1982)

Work Habits

My first notebook was a Big Five tablet, given to me by my mother with the sensible suggestion that I stop whining and learn to amuse myself by writing down my thoughts.

JOAN DIDION
Slouching Toward Bethlehem (1968)

I rewrote the ending to *Farewell to Arms*, the last page of it, thirty-nine times before I was satisfied.

ERNEST HEMINGWAY
In *Writers at Work, Second Series* (1965)

A book of mine is always a matter of life. There is something unpredictable about the process of writing, and I cannot prescribe for myself any predetermined course.

C. G. JUNG
Memories, Dreams, Reflections (1961)

First drafts are for learning what your novel or story is about. Revision is working with that knowledge to enlarge and enhance an idea, to re-form it. . . . The first draft of a book is the most uncertain—where you need guts, the ability to accept the imperfect until it is better.

BERNARD MALAMUD
In *Writers at Work, Sixth Series* (1984)

I was brought up in the great tradition of the late nineteenth century: that a writer never complains, never explains and never disdains.

JAMES MICHENER
In *The Observer* (November 26, 1989)

When I stopped writing I did not want to leave the river where I could see the trout in the pool. . . . All I must do now was stay sound and good in my head until morning when I would start to work again.

ERNEST HEMINGWAY
A Moveable Feast (1964)

For me, writing something down is the only road out.

ANNE TYLER

I had written those pages without a specific recipient in mind. For me, those were things I had inside, that occupied me and that I had to expel: tell them, indeed shout them from the roof-tops.

PRIMO LEVI
The Drowned and the Saved (1988)

I soothe my conscience now with the thought that it is better for hard words to be on paper than that Mummy should carry them in her heart.

ANNE FRANK
The Diary of a Young Girl (1958)

In all my work what I try to say is that as human beings we are more alike than we are unalike.

MAYA ANGELOU
Interview in *The New York Times* (January 20, 1993)

When I reach the heart of a story . . . the story ceases to be cold. . . . On the contrary, it becomes so alive, so important that everything I experience exists only in relation to what I'm writing. Everything I hear, see, read seems in one way or another to help my work.

Mario Vargas Llosa
Interview in *The Paris Review* (Issue 116, 1990)

I write in order to attain that feeling of tension relieved and function achieved, which a cow enjoys on giving milk.

H. L. MENCKEN

I write because I want more than one life; I insist on a wider selection. It's greed plain and simple. When my characters join the circus, I'm joining the circus. Although I'm happily married, I spent a great deal of time mentally living with incompatible husbands.

ANNE TYLER

I worked on that book [*Presumed Innocent*] for eight years on the morning commuter train and was staggered by its subsequent emergence as a best-seller. My only goal had been finally to publish a novel. I didn't even like most best-sellers, which I deemed short on imagination.

SCOTT TUROW
In *Writers on Writing:*
Collected Essays from The New York Times (2001)

I knew I must write a novel. But it seemed an impossible thing to do when I had been trying with great difficulty to write paragraphs that would be the distillation of what made a novel. It was necessary to write longer stories now as you would train for a longer race.

ERNEST HEMINGWAY
A Moveable Feast (1964)

The starting place is some kind of internal atmosphere that I want to understand. A mood. Then, I find a character who will fit that mood and call him a hero. As soon as you give your hero a goal and impediments to the goal, you've got a story going.

T. JEFFERSON PARKER
In *Writers Write: The Internet Writing Journal* (April 2003)

I do not so much write a book as sit up with it, as with a dying friend. During visiting hours, I enter its room with dread and sympathy for its many disorders. I hold its hand and hope it will get better.

Annie Dillard
The Writing Life (1989)

I write [my books] with fear, excitement, discipline, and a lot of hard work. It takes me a year to write the outline and about a month to write the first draft. But that's a matter of twenty-two-hour days. . . . All I do is write . . . the editing . . . is roughly another eighteen months.

DANIELLE STEEL
In *Snoopy's Guide to the Writing Life* (2002)

In my own writing quarter . . . I have three desks, each of a different substance and each trained to support a different activity. . . . Being able to move from desk to desk, like being able to turn over in bed, solves some cramps and fidgets and stratifies the authorial persona . . .

JOHN UPDIKE
Introduction, *The Writer's Desk* (1996)

The act of writing . . . can still provide extraordinary pleasure. For me that comes line by line at the tip of a pen, which is what I like to write with, and the pages on which the lines are written . . . can be the most valuable thing I will ever own.

JAMES SALTER
In *Why I Write: Thoughts on the Craft of Fiction* (1998)

At the purely mechanical level, impatience says I'm going to write one thousand words a day, instead of saying I'm going to write as many perfect crystallized words as possible. I know authors who stop writing their own books to write books about the difficulty of writing books.

WILLIAM F. BUCKLEY JR.
In *The Complete Guide to Writing Fiction* (1990)

What equipment you use for writing doesn't matter so long as it helps you write. On the other hand, I'd estimate that my computer, by automating routine work, has doubled my productivity, which compensates many times over for its steep initial learning curve.

RICHARD RHODES
How to Write (1995)

Over the years I have found that putting a play, or even one act, into a drawer and not looking at it for at least a few weeks makes wondrous things happen. Its faults suddenly become very clear. As I read it, what's good remains, but what's bad jumps off the page . . .

NEIL SIMON
Rewrites (1996)

I can tell you, taking eleven years to write one book is a killer financially . . . hell for your family . . . in short an inexcusable performance verging on shameful. Nevertheless, that was how long it took me to write one book, a novel called *A Man in Full.*

TOM WOLFE
Hooking Up (2000)

If it can't be read aloud, it's no good. I don't mean by this that your narrative is supposed to represent actual speech. But your prose must have the rhythms of speech . . . behind every novel is a man telling us a story face-to-face.

JOHN BRAINE
Writing a Novel (1974)

I want to make this book [*East of Eden*] so simple in its difficulty that a child can understand it. I want to go through it before it is typed and take out even the few adjectives I have let slip in.

JOHN STEINBECK
Journal of a Novel: The East of Eden *Letters* (1969)

I prefer the printout method [of revision]. . . . I find it very satisfying to be scribbling, slashing and marking up on paper. I like seeing those sentences with lines through them . . . those little carets pointing to insert-ed words and phrases. It's fun, it's play, it's making a mess in the name of art.

DAVID MICHAEL KAPLAN
Revision: A Creative Approach to Writing and Rewriting Fiction (1997)

I've never outlined a novel before starting to write it
. . . The beginnings of my novels have always been
mere flickerings in the imagination, though in each
case the flickerings have been generated, clearly
enough, by a kind of emotional ferment that had been
in process for some time.

John Hawkes
In *The Contemporary Writer* (1972)

My books have plots and subplots . . . without some
kind of literary Baedeker of my own, I would soon be
hopelessly lost. But at the same time, I try to leave a
broad area for spontaneity in my outlines . . . there is
always room for considerable creative invention as I
go along.

Irving Wallace
The Writing of One Novel (1968)

When I really know what it [the plot of a novel] is about, then I can write that end scene. I wrote the end of *Beloved* about a quarter of the way in. I wrote the end of *Jazz* very early . . . What I really want is for the plot to be *how* it happened.

Toni Morrison
In *Women Writers at Work: The Paris Review Interviews* (1998)

When I finally write that first sentence, I want to know everything that happens; so that I am not inventing the story as I write it, rather I am remembering a story. . . . The invention is over. . . . All I want to be thinking of is the language—the sentence I am writing . . . .

John Irving
My Movie Business (1999)

I'm looking for surprises as I tell a story . . . my favorite writers say that in their best stories they didn't have any idea they'd turn out the way they did. It's a good lesson . . . not to plan a story ahead of time but just to gather what's important and start out on it.

RICK BASS
In *Passion and Craft: Conversations with Notable Writers* (1998)

Since this entire structure [concept for a novel], dimly illumined in one's mind, can be compared to a painting . . . I do not go dutifully from one page to the next in consecutive order. I pick out a bit here and a bit there, till I have filled all the gaps on paper.

VLADIMIR NABOKOV
In *Playboy Interviews* (1967)

I am a writer who came of a sheltered life. A sheltered life can be a daring life as well. For all serious daring starts from within.

Eudora Welty
One Writer's Beginnings (1983)

Outlining a novel . . . gives me an understanding of the theme, the material, the main characters . . . Then, once I have a handle on the story, I don't need the outline any more. The book itself will differ in plot specifics from the outline, but it'll be the same in thrust.

ROBERT LUDLUM
In *Writing the Novel: From Plot to Print* (1979)

I observe things and remember them very accurately. It amuses me to use my powers of observation in my books and at the same time to tell people what my favorite objects are, and my favorite foods and liquors and scents, and so on.

IAN FLEMING
In *Playboy Interviews* (1967)

Now when I write I put down on the page a mere skeleton of a novel—early all my revisions are in the nature of additions, of second thoughts to make the bare bones live—but in those days to revise was to prune and prune and prune.

GRAHAM GREENE
A Sort of Life (1971)

As for my next book, I am going to hold myself from writing till I have it impending in me; grown heavy in my mind like a ripe pear; pendant, gravid, asking to be cut or it will fall.

VIRGINIA WOOLF
A Writer's Diary (1953)

4

Story, Plot, and Structure

Cracking the Danger Zone
Where Most Writers Fail

Designing story tests the maturity and insight of the writer, his knowledge of society, nature, and the human heart. Story demands both vivid imagination and powerful analytic thought . . . all stories . . . faithfully mirror their maker, exposing his humanity . . . or lack of it. Compared to this terror writing dialogue is a sweet diversion.

ROBERT McKEE
Story (1997)

Yes—oh, dear, yes—the novel tells a story.

E. M. FORSTER
Aspects of the Novel (1927)

To know what you want to say is not the best condition for writing a novel. Novels go happiest when you discover something you did not know you knew: an insight into one of your opaque characters, a metaphor that startles you . . . a truth . . . that used to elude you.

NORMAN MAILER
The Spooky Art (2003)

"You can only see as far as the headlights, but you can make the whole trip that way."

E. L. DOCTOROW
[COMPARING THE PROCESS OF WRITING A NOVEL TO DRIVING AT NIGHT.]

As the author of *The Marshall Plan for Novel Writing*, I take a structured approach to creating novels, and so I begin by creating an extremely detailed outline for my books. These outlines contain every detail I know about a story before I start writing it.

EVAN MARSHALL, AUTHOR, EDITOR, AND FOUNDER OF
THE EVAN MARSHALL AGENCY
In *Writers Write: The Internet Writing Journal*
(September 1999)

The last thing one discovers in composing a work is what to put first.

BLAISE PASCAL
Pensées (1670)

The best stories start with change . . . A stranger arrives in town. . . . The first leaves of autumn fall. . . . Notice in your reading of popular novels how often the moment of change is the moment the book begins. . . . Think deeply about how to open your story with this crucial time of threatening change.

JACK M. BICKHAM
Writing and Selling Your Novel (1996)

A strong enough situation renders the whole question of plot moot, which is fine with me. The most interesting situations can usually be expressed as a *What-if* question: *What if* vampires invaded a small New England village? [*Salem's Lot*]

STEPHEN KING
On Writing (2000)

In nearly all good fiction, the basic—all but inescapable—plot form is: *A central character wants something, goes after it despite opposition (perhaps including his own doubts), and so arrives at a win, lose, or draw.*

JOHN GARDNER
On Becoming a Novelist (1983)

There is a flip side to narrative tension. While it pulls the reader into the book and holds her there, it simultaneously imposes on the writer the need to get on with the story. It works to inhibit tangential meanderings and self-indulgent interludes that eat at a reader's time.

SUSAN RABINER AND ALFRED FORTUNATO
Thinking Like Your Editor (2002)

It seems to me that when a writer is successful in using a story taken from experience, it is not told exactly the way it happened, but in the way that reveals, through all one's beliefs, hopes and fears, how the event should have happened.

CRAIG NOVA
In *The Writing Life:*
Collection from Washington Post Book World (2003)

Plot must further the novel towards its object. What object? The non-poetic statement of a poetic truth. Have not all poetic truths been already stated? The essence of a poetic truth is that no statement of it can be final.

ELIZABETH BOWEN
Collected Impressions (1950)

No matter which fictional form [novel or short story] you are using, you are writing a story, and in a story something has to happen. A perception is not a story, and no amount of sensitivity can make a story-writer out of you if you just plain don't have a gift for telling a story.

FLANNERY O'CONNOR
In *Mystery and Manners* (1969)

———

An intricate plot design that pre-exists the work itself is not going to result in an organic work of the imagination. I'm not saying I don't *try* to figure out what I'm doing, but usually I only figure it out by doing it. That's the excitement of writing.

JAY MCINERNEY
In *On Being a Writer* (1989)

If you start fumbling around with plot, you're lost. Plot is the great boogey-man of the writer's journey, because it can be made to seem esoteric. It isn't esoteric at all. It is automatic. It will appear in the company of sustained conflict.

JACK WOODFORD
Writer's Cramp (1953)

Constructing a novel—telling a tale, for me at any rate—is not a business of thinking of a story, arranging it in a certain order, and then finding images to fit it. The images come first . . . *The situation, somehow, must be made to rise out of the image.*

PAUL SCOTT
On Writing and the Novel (1987)

All the people they [readers] envy in my books . . .
they have to come to a bad end, see, because that way
the people who read me can get off the subway and go
home feeling better about their own crappy lives and
luckier than the people they've been reading about.

JACQUELINE SUSANN
In *Another Life* (1999)

Persons attempting to find a motive in this narrative will be prosecuted; persons attempting to find a moral in it will be banished; persons attempting to find a plot in it will be shot.

MARK TWAIN
The Adventures of Huckleberry Finn (1884)

Scene is only justified in the novel where it can be shown, or at least felt, to act upon action or character. In fact, where it has dramatic use.

When not intended for dramatic use, scene is a sheer slower-down. Its staticness is a dead weight.

ELIZABETH BOWEN
Collected Impressions (1950)

One sentence. Two at most. If you can't tell yourself what your story is in one or two sentences, you're already running into trouble. Even in *Moby Dick*, it comes down to *Captain Ahab chases a whale and doesn't get it.*

GERALD PETIEVICH
In *The Writer's Digest Handbook of Novel Writing* (1992)

I learned early on, from all the plays I had seen or read, that every play must be about an event. Like the first time "something" has ever happened . . . a major event in the lives of the leading characters. In . . . *[Barefoot in the Park]* . . . it was the first day of the newly-wed couple.

NEIL SIMON
Rewrites (1996)

The theme, the "meaning" of a story, is not something you can sit down and plan out ahead of time. . . . Theme should grow from your characters and your plot, naturally, almost subconsciously. If you sit down to deliver a Great Message . . . *above all else* . . . then you are an essayist, not a novelist.

DEAN R. KOONTZ
Writing Popular Fiction (1972)

If I didn't know the ending of a story, I wouldn't begin. I always write my last lines, my last paragraph, my last page first, and then I go back and work towards it. I know where I'm going. . . . And how I get there is God's grace.

KATHERINE ANNE PORTER
In *Writers at Work, Second Series* (1965)

I do my plotting in my head as I go along, and usually I do it wrong and have to do it all over again. . . . With me plots are not made, they grow. And if they refuse to grow, you throw the stuff away and start over again.

RAYMOND CHANDLER
In *Raymond Chandler Speaking* (1977)

5

The Insiders

---

*Publishers, Editors,
and Agents*

It was always a common joke among publishing people that "this would be a great business if it weren't for writers," but by the mid-seventies publishing was beginning to be run by people who at heart believed that and included editors as well.

MICHAEL KORDA
Another Life (1999)

Though our publishers will tell you that they are ever seeking "original" writers, nothing could be farther from the truth. What they want is more of the same, only thinly disguised. They most certainly do not want another Faulkner . . . Melville. . . . What the *public* wants, no one knows. Not even the publishers.

HENRY MILLER
"When I Reach for My Revolver" (1955)

"F__k 'em! I don't write for middle-aged men in suits.
I write for women on the subway."

Jacqueline Susann

In *The Writing Life:*
Collection from Washington Post Book World (2003)

[Susann's response after being warned that one of the book clubs might not take one of her novels, *The Love Machine*, because the management was afraid it was too shocking. They eventually took the book.]

Most editors will only acquire a short-story collection when it comes contractually attached to a novel. . . . "When I offer to give books to friends who don't work in the business," an editor told me, "it's really striking how they lose interest when you tell them it's a book of short stories."

SUE MILLER
"Long Story Short", in *The New York Times Book Review* (November 2, 2003)

Even the most cynical editors realize that it can take writers a long time to hit their stride. Authors like Martin Cruz Smith and Marion Zimmer Bradley published scores of paperbacks and were around for decades before finally producing the hardcover bestsellers (*Gorky Park* and *The Mists of Avalon* respectively) that made them famous.

> RUSSELL GALEN
> In *The Writer's Digest Handbook of Novel Writing* (1992)

By the nature of their profession they [editors] read too much, with the result that they grow jaded and cannot see talent when it dances in front of them.

> JOHN GARDNER
> *On Becoming a Novelist* (1983)

The New Yorker will be the magazine which is not edited for the old lady in Dubuque.

HAROLD ROSS, ATTRIBUTED

In *The Years with Ross* (1957)

[THE *New Yorker* PROSPECTUS (1924) SEVERAL MONTHS BEFORE THE FIRST PUBLICATION OF THE MAGAZINE IN 1925. THIS QUOTE IS OFTEN ATTRIBUTED TO LEGENDARY *New Yorker* EDITOR HAROLD ROSS, WHO WAS ONE OF THE TEN ADVISORY EDITORS WHO WORKED ON THE PROSPECTUS.]

Just get in down on paper, and then we'll see what to do with it.

MAXWELL PERKINS
Advice to Marcia Davenport

Try to preserve an author's style if he is an author and has a style. Try to make dialogue sound like talk, not writing.

WALCOTT GIBBS
In *The Years with Ross* (1957)

An editor is one who separates the wheat from the chaff and prints the chaff.

ADLAI STEVENSON
The Stevenson Wit (1966)

Graham Greene, whom I would eventually publish for nearly twenty years, neither needed nor accepted editorial changes. When [a previous publisher] had expressed some doubt about the title of one of Greene's books, he had received a terse cable in reply that read: "EASIER TO CHANGE PUBLISHER THAN TITLE. GREENE."

MICHAEL KORDA, PUBLISHER
In *The Writing Life:*
Collection from Washington Post Book World (2003)

Yes, I suppose that some editors are failed writers—but so are most writers.

T. S. ELIOT
[HIS REMARK TO PUBLISHER ROBERT GIROUX]

Most editors, with some notable exceptions, have become packagers now, rather than close editors. And I think that publishers are more interested in acquisitions from their editors than they are in developing to the fullest extent the craft of each writer they deal with.

JOHN HERSEY
In *Writers at Work: The Paris Review Interviews, Eighth Series* (1988)

The second-to-last draft of *The Great Gatsby*—the version Fitzgerald turned in to his editor, Maxwell Perkins—has been published in a revealing scholarly edition that shows exactly how, partly by using Perkins's suggestions, Fitzgerald was able to transform a good novel into a great one.

STEPHEN KOCH
The Modern Library Writer's Workshop: A Guide to the Craft of Fiction (2003)
[THE BOOK REFERENCED IS *Trimalchio: An Early Version of* THE GREAT GATSBY, JAMES L. W. WEST III, EDITOR. CAMBRIDGE UNIVERSITY PRESS.]

I was not, he said, a Flaubert kind of writer . . . not a perfectionist. I had . . . any number of books in me, and the important thing was to get them produced and not to spend the rest of my life in perfecting one book . . .

THOMAS WOLFE
The Story of a Novel (1935)
[COMMENTING ON HIS EDITOR MAX PERKINS]

Some writers like a good deal of help from their editors, others, like myself reject it. Editors inhabit the publishing world, have lunch and cocktails together, and represent the opinions and attitudes of their class. Or its prejudices.

SAUL BELLOW
In *The Contemporary Writer* (1972)

Good editors are really the third eye. Cool. Dispassionate. They don't love you or your work; for me that is what is valuable—not compliments. Sometimes it's uncanny; the editor puts his or her finger on exactly the place the writer knows is weak. . . .

TONI MORRISON

In *Women Writers at Work: The Paris Review Interviews* (1998)

Outsiders, particularly from the West Coast, used to say how nice it must be to work in a business where people weren't crazy and where greed and ego were at least kept to rational levels, but by the 1970s they were wrong.

MICHAEL KORDA
Another Life (1999)

To this he answered that the book was not only finished, but that if I took six months more on it, I would then demand another six months and six months more beyond that. . . .

THOMAS WOLFE
The Story of a Novel (1935)
[AFTER EXTENSIVE SESSIONS WITH MAX PERKINS CUTTING TENS
OF THOUSANDS OF WORDS FROM HIS *Of Time and the River*
MANUSCRIPT, WHILE AT THE SAME TIME DOING CONSIDERABLE
ADDITIONS AND REWRITING, WOLFE INSISTED THE BOOK WAS NOT
FINISHED AND BEGGED PERKINS FOR SIX MORE MONTHS' WORK
ON IT.]

Nobody gives a damn about a writer or his problems except another writer.

HAROLD ROSS
In *The Years with Ross* (1957)

There could be nothing so important as a book can be.

MAXWELL PERKINS
In Maxwell Perkins: Editor of Genius (1978)

It's a damn good story. If you have any comments write them on the back of a check.

EARLE STANLEY GARDNER
In *Good Advice on Writing* (1992)
[FROM GARDNER'S NOTE TO THE EDITOR ON A MANUSCRIPT]

Changing agents is like changing deck chairs on the *Titanic.*

OLD WRITING AND PUBLISHING BROMIDE

When I have spoken at writers conferences, I have been dismayed by how many new writers are obsessed with getting an agent . . . it is a serious mistake for new writers to expend as much energy searching for representation as they expend creating their books.

DEAN R. KOONTZ
In *The Writer's Digest Handbook of Novel Writing* (1992)

In query letters [seeking an agent] many writers immediately put themselves down, and they don't even know they're doing it. They'll tell me in the first paragraph how long they've been trying to get published without any success, how countless agents have already rejected their manuscript. . . . The sad story does *not* impress agents.

JEFF HERMAN, THE JEFF HERMAN AGENCY
In *Writers Write: The Internet Writing Journal*
(February 2000)

Writers should learn to write good query letters. They should stop trying to be cute and attention-getting and understand that a query letter is simply a business letter in which a writer describes her [or his] project and credentials and asks whether the agent would like to consider the work in question.

EVAN MARSHALL, THE EVAN MARSHALL AGENCY
In *Writers Write: The Internet Writing Journal*
(September 1999)

Look at the books that you feel are similar in nature, atmosphere or tone to what you are writing and see who publishes them. See if they have thanked an editor and/or agent in the book. And if they have, send a letter. Target the agent first. . . .

JENNIFER SAWYER FISHER, SENIOR EDITOR, AVON BOOKS
In *Writers Write: The Internet Writing Journal* (April 1999)

Writers are like mushrooms: They're fed a lot of horseshit and kept in the dark.

AGENT RICHARD CURTIS, QUOTING A CLIENT
In *Honk if You're a Writer* (1992)

Writers with three chapters of a novel completed should be glued to the novel. Writers with six short stories should be developing their craft, their stamina, their imagination, and their portfolios. *First you become a writer; then you contact an agent.*

LEONARD S. BERNSTEIN
Getting Published: The Writer in the Combat Zone (1986)

What catches my eye in a new mystery manuscript is impeccable writing . . . and a strikingly original "hook." The hook is a fresh and interesting occupation for the sleuth, a setting or time period we haven't seen before, or some other aspect that sets the book apart . . .

EVAN MARSHALL, EVAN MARSHALL AGENCY
In *Writers Write: The Internet Writing Journal*
(September 1999)

6

The Ups and Downs of the Writing Life

————

*Rejection, Success, and the
Quest to Make It*

What a heavy oar the pen is, and what a strong current ideas are to row in.

GUSTAVE FLAUBERT
Letter (1851)

What happens to a blocked writer is this: not only is he unable to finish anything he starts, but after a while he literally forgets how to write, becoming tangled in syntax and lost in grammar . . . there is nothing to do but stop . . .

NORMAN PODHORETZ
Making It (1967)

Giving birth to a book is always an abominable torture for me, because it cannot answer my imperious need for universality and totality.

EMILE ZOLA

I think I may boast myself to be, with all possible vanity, the most unlearned and uninformed female who ever dared to be an authoress.

JANE AUSTEN

The novel is like the Great Bitch in one's life. We think we're rid of her, we go on to other women . . . we're enjoying ourselves . . . we'll never suffer her depressions again, and then we turn a corner . . . and there's the Bitch smiling at us, and we're trapped.

NORMAN MAILER
The Spooky Art (2003)

It has taken me years of struggle, hard work and research to learn to make one simple gesture, and I know enough about the art of writing to realize that it would take as many years of concentrated effort to write one simple beautiful sentence.

ISADORA DUNCAN

You don't say, "I've done it!" You come, with a kind of horrible desperation, to realize that this will do.

ANTHONY BURGESS
The Agony and the Ego (1993)

Quality cannot be considered a constant. It does not pour forth relentlessly, unabated. It is not a constant for the beginning writer and it is not a constant for the top-flight professional. The difference is that the professionals know this and accept it.

LEONARD S. BERNSTEIN
Getting Published: The Writer in the Combat Zone (1986)

Crime does not pay—enough.

CLAYTON RAWSON, FOUNDER, MYSTERY WRITERS OF AMERICA
In *American Heritage Dictionary of American Quotations*
(1997)

There are some things which cannot be learned quickly and time, which is all we have, must be paid heavily for their acquiring.

ERNEST HEMINGWAY
Death in the Afternoon (1932)

How can you hate the actual writing? What is there to hate about it? How can you hate the magic which makes a paragraph or a sentence or a line of dialogue or a description something in the nature of a new creation?

RAYMOND CHANDLER
In *Raymond Chandler Speaking* (1977)

Don't ask a writer what he's working on. It's like asking someone with cancer about the progress of his disease.

JAY MCINERNEY
Brightness Falls (1992)

To begin with, [writing a book] is a toy and an amusement. Then it becomes a mistress, then it becomes a master, then it becomes a tyrant. The last phase is that just as you are about to be reconciled to your servitude, you kill the monster and fling it to the public.

WINSTON CHURCHILL
In *The New York Times Magazine* (November 13, 1949)

The "illumination" only occurs during the work. It's the hard work that, at any given time, can unleash that . . . heightened perception, that excitement capable of bringing about revelation, solution, and light.

MARIO VARGAS LLOSA
In *The Paris Review* (Issue 116, 1990)

Writing is easy. All you have to do is sit at a typewriter and open a vein.

RED SMITH, ATTRIBUTED

There's one other kind of writer's block, and that's the discovery that what you set out to do isn't worth the effort. That's a different kind of block, when you find out it isn't worth the time you're putting into it.

Tom Wolfe
Interview by Steve Hammer (1998)

———•••••———

A writer's block is most often caused by one of five things: overwork, boredom, self-doubt, financial worries, or emotional problems between the writer and those close to him.

Dean R. Koontz
Writing Popular Fiction (1972)

Yet having stopped, he [the blocked writer] can never know if the block has disappeared unless he tries to write again, and so he goes on trying, only to be defeated again and again and plunged deeper and deeper into self-hating despair. . . .

NORMAN PODHORETZ
Making It (1967)

The books I most long to write are precisely those for which I am least endowed. *Bovary,* in this sense, is an unprecedented tour de force . . . Writing this book I am like a man playing the piano with leaden balls attached to his fingers.

GUSTAVE FLAUBERT
Letter to Louise Colet (1852)

Now I have sat a week. It is Friday and I have sweated out one page and a half. If I did not know this process so well, I would consider it a week of waste. But . . . I am content. . . . In fact, I feel a great gain.

JOHN STEINBECK
Journal of a Novel: The East of Eden *Letters* (1969)

How hellishing wide of the mark I write most of the time. . . . If we get on paper the real vividness and heat of what went racing through our minds we'd begin to be actual storytellers. It's a discouraging business.

ERNEST HAYCOX
In *Ernest Haycox* (1996)

A thing may in itself be the finest piece of writing one has ever done, and yet have absolutely no place in the manuscript one hopes to publish. That is a hard thing, but it must be faced, and so we faced it. . . . My spirit quivered at the bloody execution.

THOMAS WOLFE
The Story of a Novel (1935)
[ON FINALLY REALIZING, THROUGH LEGENDARY EDITOR MAXWELL PERKINS OF SCRIBNERS, THAT HIS 100,000-WORD INTRODUCTORY CHAPTER TO *Of Time and the River* COULD NOT POSSIBLY STAY IN THE NOVEL, AS WRITTEN.]

It's hostile [the act of writing] in that you're trying to make somebody see something the way you see it, trying to impose your idea, your picture. . . . Quite often you want to tell somebody your dream, your nightmare. . . . The writer is always tricking the reader into listening to the dream.

JOAN DIDION

In *Women Writers at Work: The Paris Review Interviews* (1998)

Brief subjects require brief treatments. There is *nothing* so difficult as a novel, as anyone knows who has attempted one; a short story is bliss to write set beside a novel of even ordinary proportions.

JOYCE CAROL OATES

In *Women Writers at Work: The Paris Review Interviews* (1998)

I have spent many months on a first paragraph and once I get it, the rest comes out very easily. In the first paragraph you solve most of the problems with your book. The theme is defined, the style, the tone.

GABRIEL GARCIA MARQUEZ
In *Writers at Work, Sixth Series* (1984)

I had a ten-page outline [*The Godfather*]—but nobody would take me. Months went by. I was working on a string of adventure magazines, editing, writing free-lance stories . . . I was ready to forget novels except maybe as a puttering hobby for old age.

MARIO PUZO
The Godfather Papers (1972)

Your manuscript is both good and original, but the part that is good is not original, and the part that is original is not good.

SAMUEL JOHNSON
In *Rotten Rejections* (1990)

———

"Sorry, but the majority here feel that The Back of a Bear *is not a St. Vitus book. Know I was your good and willing advocate. Cordially, Amos Gotfodgett"*. . . . Ten months . . . [he] had held my manuscript while building up my hopes the better to dash them in twenty five words or less.

LARRY L. KING
None but a Blockhead (1986)

...and the year worrying about money *(all of the stories back in the mail that came in through a slit in the saw-mill door, with notes of rejection that would never call them stories, but always anecdotes, sketches, contes, etc. They did not want them . . .)*

ERNEST HEMINGWAY
Green Hills of Africa (1935)

Tom Heggen's first novel, *Mister Roberts*, was not rejected. It was published . . . by Houghton Mifflin, in 1946, and became a bestseller at once; in 1948 it was turned into a smash hit play. In May 1949 Heggen took an overdose of pills and drowned himself.

JOHN WHITE
Rejection (1982)

I sent . . . a query letter [for the novel *Flight of the Intruder*]. But all I got were rejections. Then I saw *Hunt for Red October* in the bookstores, and decided to send my manuscript to that publisher—the Naval Institute Press. They called me up and said they'd like to publish it. After it hit the bestseller list [*N.Y. Times*, 28 weeks] . . . I never looked back.

STEPHEN COONTS
In *Writers Write: The Internet Writing Journal* (January 2000)

Nothing stinks like a pile of unpublished writing.

SYLVIA PLATH
The Bell Jar (1963)

John Kennedy Toole wrote a comic novel about life in New Orleans called *A Confederacy of Dunces*. It was so relentlessly rejected ... that he killed himself ... His mother refused to give up . . . got it accepted by the Louisiana State University Press, and . . . it won the Pulitzer Prize for fiction.

In *Rotten Rejections* (1990)

I ... found that the book I had just published had been given a bad review . . . there were a lot of other bad reviews, too. There is no silence like the silence that comes from a publisher when things are going badly. No paperback book sale. I was broke.

CRAIG NOVA
Brook Trout and the Writing Life (1999)

Some of the editors wrote rejection slips that were more creative than anything I had written. On my tenth submission to *Redbook* . . . "Mrs. Clark, your stories are light, slight, and trite." My first novella was returned with the succinct note: "We found the heroine as boring as her husband had."

MARY HIGGINS CLARK
In *The Writing Life:
Collection from Washington Post Book World* (2003)

Irving Stone's first book was about Van Gogh. He took it to Alfred Knopf, and "they never opened it—the package with the manuscript got home before I did." After fifteen more rejections the book, *Lust for Life,* was finally accepted and published in 1934. It has now sold about twenty-five million copies.

In *Rotten Rejections* (1990)

Ross Lockridge's first novel, *Raintree County,* was never rejected. Houghton Mifflin published it in January, 1948 and on February 27 Lockridge got word that it had become the country's number one best-seller; on March 6 he asphyxiated himself.

JOHN WHITE
Rejection (1982)

According to legend, *Gone With the Wind* survived thirty-eight [rejections]. (Very much "according to legend"—according to Burke Wilkinson [an author of eleven successful books] . . . "Harold Latham, the conscientious editor at Macmillan, learned about GWTW early, commuted to Atlanta to keep Margaret Mitchell tracking, and truly no other firm ever saw the manuscript.")

JOHN WHITE
Rejection (1982)
[THE LEGEND THAT *Gone With the Wind* HAD BEEN REJECTED SEVERAL TIMES IS ONE THIS EDITOR HAS HEARD MANY TIMES IN HIS LIFE WITH GREAT DISBELIEF. IT JUST DOESN'T SEEM POSSIBLE. AND TODAY WE KNOW: IT NEVER HAPPENED! FOR MORE INFORMATION ON THE SUBJECT, SEE THE WEB SITE, "MARGARET MITCHELL: THE CREATOR OF A LEGEND." www.ttelracs/gwtw2.htm]

The shelf life of the modern hardback writer is somewhere between the milk and the yoghurt.

JOHN MORTIMER

—◆—

If you write compulsively, you wait, quivering, for one thing: the moment you are finally paid for something you've written. Then you're anointed—a "real" writer. Before that validation, you feel like you're looking across a forbidding medieval moat, and everybody but you is inside the castle, partying.

LESLIE DIXON
In *Snoopy's Guide to the Writing Life* (2002)

Nobody becomes Tom Wolfe overnight, not even Tom Wolfe.

WILLIAM ZINSSER
On Writing Well: An Informal Guide to Writing Nonfiction
(1980)

———•——•——

The principle . . . we must hold if we are to survive as writers, deluded or otherwise: even when all evidence is to the contrary, *we are steadily improving; whatever we are working on at the present time is the best thing we have ever done, and the next book will be even better.*

JOYCE CAROL OATES
Woman Writer: Occasions and Opportunities (1988)

Sir, no man but a blockhead ever wrote except for money.

> SAMUEL JOHNSON
> In *Life of Johnson* (1791)

Good writers define reality; bad ones merely restate it. A good writer turns fact into truth; a bad writer will, more often than not, accomplish the opposite.

> EDWARD F. ALBEE
> In *The Saturday Review* (May 4, 1966)

With each book you write you should lose the admirers you gained with the previous one.

> ANDRÉ GIDE

Best-sellers are about murder, money, revenge, ambition, and sex; sex, sex. So are literary novels. But best-selling authors give you more per page: there are five murders, three world financial crises, two bankruptcies and a civil war in *A Dangerous Fortune.*

> KEN FOLLETT
> *The Writer's Companion* (1996)

In a sobering cartoon that appeared some years ago, a beggar works a street corner with tin cup and a sign that reads:

SOLD ONE STORY, QUIT MY JOB

. . . Yes, it's a stupid fantasy, and most people know better—including those who seem to have achieved writer's nirvana.

> ARTHUR PLOTNIK
> *Honk if You're a Writer* (1992)

He's taking the nylon cover off his Texas Instruments desk calculator . . . about to measure the flow, the tide, the mad sluice, the crazy current of money that pours through his fingers every month and which is now running against him in the most catastrophic manner, like an undertow, a riptide. . . .

TOM WOLFE
Mauve Gloves and Madmen, Clutter and Vine (1976)

I greeted the mailman one morning and discovered a check for more than $46,000 as my take for a mere one week [for the play *The Best Little Whorehouse in Texas*]. I tried to develop a decent sense of shame . . . No, by God, I had paid my dues: taking odd jobs as a delivery boy and a busboy when almost forty years old. . . .

LARRY L. KING
None but a Blockhead (1986)

Roger Simon, a fine mystery writer, once gave a wonderful speech, in which he said: The success of any of your friends is a genuine cause for rejoicing, because it brings you closer to the charmed circle of people who are doing their best work and having a good time.

CAROLYN SEE
Making a Literary Life:
Advice for Writers and Other Dreamers (2002)

The common idea that success spoils people by making them vain, egotistic, and self-complacent is erroneous; on the contrary it makes them, for the most part, humble, tolerant, and kind. Failure makes people bitter and cruel.

W. SOMERSET MAUGHAM
The Summing Up (1938)

Only a year and a half ago did I realize what had happened to me as a result of *The Lost Weekend*—its ballooning to a success out of all proportion to its real value. You feel a fraud. I know that Thomas Heggen felt that way; he was scared to death.

CHARLES JACKSON
In *The Writer Observed* (1956)
[THOMAS HEGGEN COMMITTED SUICIDE AFTER THE SUCCESS OF HIS NOVEL AND PLAY *Mister Roberts*.]

It took me fifteen years to discover that I had no talent for writing, but I couldn't give it up because by that time I was too famous.

ROBERT BENCHLEY
Benchley Beside Himself (1943)

The great thing is to last and get your work done and see and hear and learn and understand; and write when there is something that you know; and not before; and not too damned much after.

ERNEST HEMINGWAY
Death in the Afternoon (1932)

It wasn't just the writing that counted, but a writing life. Dedication, endurance, passion, idealism, daring, strength, dignity, a respect and responsibility toward your gift. These were not relics from a romantic age, but pragmatic qualities a writer still needed, those and a certain way of looking at life . . .

W. D. WETHERELL
North of Now (1998)

I was forty-five years old and tired of being an artist. Besides, I owed $20,000. . . . I had been a true believer in art . . . It gave me a comfort I found in no other place. But I knew I'd never be able to write another book if the next one wasn't a success.

MARIO PUZO

The Godfather Papers (1972)

[PUZO DESCRIBING HIS SENSE OF FAILURE AFTER WRITING TWO NOVELS, *The Dark Arena* (1955) AND *The Fortunate Pilgrim* (1965) THAT WERE CRITICALLY PRAISED BUT COMMERCIAL FLOPS.]

The only poets with full-time salaries earn them at greeting-card companies.

BILL THOMAS

In *Los Angeles Times* (January 13, 1991)

7

Hollywood

Of Money and Misery

All writers are schmucks with Underwoods.

JACK WARNER, PRODUCER, ATTRIBUTED

———

[Writers today who write for money] cannot afford to ignore the sucking pull of Hollywood's massive case machine. Duh, but do I have to mention that magazines don't pay that well. . . . As for novels, my standard line is: I was looking for a lower-paying profession than journalism, so I took up novel writing.

MARK JACOBSON
In *Why I Write: Thoughts on the Craft of Fiction* (1998)

I read part of it all the way through.

SAMUEL GOLDWYN, ATTRIBUTED

Why write, when you can watch a movie on your typewriter?

ROY BLOUNT JR.
In *The Writer's Desk* (1996)

WILL YOU ACCEPT THREE HUNDRED PER WEEK TO WORK FOR PARAMOUNT PICTURES? ALL EXPENSES PAID. THE THREE HUNDRED IS PEANUTS. MILLIONS ARE TO BE MADE OUT HERE AND YOUR ONLY COMPETITION IS IDIOTS. DON'T LET THIS GET AROUND.

JOSEPH MANKIEWICZ
In *Writers in Hollywood* (1990)
Telegram to Ben Hecht

I would rather take a fifty-mile hike than crawl through a book.

JACK WARNER, ATTRIBUTED

If your dream were to compose music, would you say to yourself, "I've heard a lot of symphonies . . . I can also play the piano . . . I think I'll knock one out this weekend"? No. But that's exactly how many screen-writers begin. "I've seen a lot of flicks . . . I got A's in English . . . vacation time's coming . . . "

ROBERT MCKEE
Story (1997)

The trouble with Hollywood is that there are too many geniuses and not enough men of talent.

ROBERT NATHAN
In *The Writer Observed* (1956)

⸺

My chief memory of movieland is one of asking in the producers' office why I must change the script, eviscerate it, cripple and hamstring it? . . . Half of the movie writers argue in this fashion. The other half writhe in silence, and the psychoanalysts' couch or the liquor bottle claim them both.

BEN HECHT
In *Writers in Hollywood* (1990)

You see, it brings out that uncomfortable little thing called conscience. You aren't writing for the love of it or the art of it . . . you are doing a chore . . . you have to live with yourself. You don't—or at least, only in highly exceptional circumstances—have to live with your producer.

DOROTHY PARKER
In *Writers in Hollywood* (1990)

I was convinced in the beginning that there must be some discoverable method of working in pictures which would not be completely stultifying . . . I discovered that was a dream. Too many people have too much to say about a writer's work. It ceases to be his own.

RAYMOND CHANDLER
In *Raymond Chandler Speaking* (1977)

I was approaching what I believe to be the single most important lesson to be learned about writing for films and this is it:

SCREENPLAYS ARE STRUCTURE

WILLIAM GOLDMAN
Adventures in the Screen Trade (1983)

No, No, No, No, No, No, No, No, No, No, No, No, No, No, No, No, No, No, No O'Neill

EUGENE O'NEILL
In *American Literary Anecdotes* (1990)
[ANSWERING A CABLE REQUESTING THAT O'NEILL WRITE A
SCREENPLAY FOR A JEAN HARLOW FILM. THE CABLE INCLUDED
A NOTE TO CONFINE HIS COLLECT REPLY TO TWENTY WORDS
OR LESS.]

The hardest thing for a novelist to learn [about screenplay writing] is that you first have to see the frame and then let the words follow. So much of the novel is made up of what people are thinking and there the language properly comes first.

JIM HARRISON
Off to the Side: A Memoir (2002)

Most novelists, I believe, harbor the secret belief that they can easily toss off screenplays, rather as most sports fans believe themselves to be potential athletes. Unlike armchair athletes, however, armchair screenwriters . . . are often allowed to professionalize their fantasy—which for the most part they do flounderingly.

LARRY MCMURTRY
Film Flam: Essays on Hollywood (1987)

Bestowing the award for the most odious person you ever knew in Hollywood isn't the sort of thing you rush into; you're faced, so to speak, with an embarrassment of riches.

S. J. PERELMAN
The Last Laugh (1981)

And then there's the one about the aspiring Polish movie starlet. She comes to Hollywood, and the first thing she does is sleep with a writer.

OLD HOLLYWOOD WRITING JOKE

Some [screenwriters making pitches] tried to condense their ideas to twenty-five words, in and out, as they'd learned in some screenwriting class . . . They'd talk about the "arc of the story." They'd use little code words and phrases like *paradigm* and *first-act bump.*

MICHAEL TOLKIN
The Player (1988)

Storytelling in screenplays follows a much more ruthless course than in novels. . . . In a novel, there is no reason all the characters can't be as fully developed (and/or sympathetic) as the writer chooses. . . . In a film you're always fighting the constraints of time. There are characters who will be given short shrift.

JOHN IRVING
My Movie Business (1999)

I doubt if there are proportionately any more first-rate novels than good movies in a particular year, but given the intelligentsia's scorn of Hollywood, this is not an acceptable idea. . . . I have also noted evidence that some of the loathing for Hollywood is a veiled form of anti-Semitism. . . .

JIM HARRISON
In *Why I Write: Thoughts on the Craft of Fiction* (1998)

Nothing can injure a man's writing if he's a first-rate writer. If a man is not a first-rate writer, there's not anything can help it much. The problem does not apply if he is not first rate, because he has already sold his soul for a swimming pool.

WILLIAM FAULKNER
In *Writers at Work* (1958)
[ANSWERING THE QUESTION: CAN WORKING FOR THE MOVIES HURT YOUR OWN WRITING?]

The transition I was able to make from writing fiction to making movies was a case not of graduating from one to the other, . . . but of . . . another kind of story-telling I'd always been interested in. Ideas for stories usually come to me in their own form—short story, play, novel, movie.

JOHN SAYLES
Thinking in Pictures (1987)

Yes, nifty dialog helps one hell of a lot; sure, it's nice if you can bring your characters to life. But you can have terrific characters spouting just swell talk to each other, and if the structure is unsound, forget it.

WILLIAM GOLDMAN
Adventures in the Screen Trade (1983)

The potential for solidity in movies, their ability to make you feel the tangible weight of objects, the immediate consequences of actions, has something to do with why some stories present themselves as movies and some don't.

JOHN SAYLES
Thinking in Pictures (1987)

Writing may have comparatively little to do with how a movie turns out. Direction, acting, casting, cutting, photography, pacing, lighting, mood, sound, special effects, technical competence or the lack of it—all may be more important than the writing. Certainly Hollywood thinks so.

LARRY L. KING
None but a Blockhead (1986)

The printed word cannot compete with the movies on their ground, and should not. You can describe beautiful faces, car chases, or valleys full of Indians on horseback . . . and you will not approach the movies' spectacle. Novels written with film contracts in mind have a faint but unmistakable, and ruinous, odor.

ANNIE DILLARD
The Writing Life (1989)

8

The Critics

Ouch!

You can spot the bad critic when he starts by discussing the poet and not the poem.

EZRA POUND
The ABCs of Reading (1934)

One cannot review a bad book without showing off.

W. H. AUDEN
The Dyer's Hand (1962)

The reason why so few good books are written is that so few people who can write know anything.

WALTER BAGEHOT

Another damned, thick, square book! Always, scribble, scribble, scribble! Eh! Mr. Gibbon?

THE DUKE OF GLOUCESTER, BROTHER OF KING GEORGE III
[To EDWARD GIBBON WHEN PRESENTED WITH A SECOND VOLUME OF *History of the Decline and Fall of the Roman Empire* IN 1786. THE FIRST VOLUME HAD APPEARED IN 1776.]

If they [writers] believe the critics when they say they are great then they must believe them when they say they are rotten and they lose confidence.

ERNEST HEMINGWAY
Green Hills of Africa (1935)

Neil Simon didn't have an idea for a play this year but he wrote it anyway.

WALTER KERR
In *The New York Times* (1996)
[HIS REVIEW OF SIMON'S *The Star-Spangled Girl.*]

A "smartcracker" they called me, and that makes me sick and unhappy. There's a hell of a distance between wisecracking and wit. Wit has truth in it; wisecracking is simply calisthenics with words.

DOROTHY PARKER
In *Writers at Work* (1958)

A man is a critic when he cannot be an artist, in the same way that a man becomes an informer when he cannot be a soldier.

GUSTAVE FLAUBERT
Letter to Louise Colet (1846)

A good writer is not per se a good book critic. No more than a good drunk is automatically a good bartender.

JIM BISHOP
In *New York Journal-American* (November 1957)

———

The test of a good critic is when he knows when and how to believe in insufficient evidence.

SAMUEL BUTLER

———

The practice of "reviewing" . . . in general has nothing in common with the art of criticism.

HENRY JAMES
Criticism (1893)

Once, on the word of my agent . . . I tore up a whole book and burned it . . . [He] had remarked of this enormous volume (of which I was quite proud) as follows: "It seems to me you may have written an elaborate treatment of a book you may have had in mind to write some day."

ROBERT RUARK
In *The Lost Classics of Robert Ruark* (1996)

If behind the erratic gunfire of . . . [professional critics] the author felt that there was another kind of criticism, the opinion of people reading for the love of reading, slowly and unprofessionally, and judging with great sympathy and yet with great severity, might this not improve the quality of his work?

VIRGINIA WOOLF
The Second Common Reader (1932)

Let them keep reminding their friends not to read you—you just keep coming back at them with your imagination, and give up on giving them, thirty years too late, the speech of the good boy at the synagogue.

PHILIP ROTH
The Facts (1988)

I regard reviews as a kind of infant's disease to which newborn books are subject.

GEORG CHRISTOPH LICHTENBERG

Asking a working writer what he thinks about critics is like asking a lamppost what it feels about dogs.

CHRISTOPHER HAMPTON
In *Sun Times Magazine* (October 16, 1977)

———

Little old ladies of both sexes.

JOHN O'HARA
In *The New York Times Book Review* (January 6, 1985)

Nature fits all her children with something to do,
He who would write and can't write, can surely review.

JAMES RUSSELL LOWELL
A Fable for Critics (1848)

I write fiction and I'm told [by critics] it's autobiography, I write autobiography and I'm told it's fiction, so since I'm so dim and they're so smart, let *them* decide what it is or isn't.

PHILIP ROTH
Deception (1990)

They [writers] fret over savage reviews because rejection of their work . . . means rejection of themselves and of years of their working lives . . . However, it is clear that no review, no matter how bad or how unfair, can seriously injure the sale of a book if the public desires to read it.

IRVING WALLACE
The Writing of One Novel (1968)

They [critics] have claimed for themselves the task of being intermediaries between the author and the reader. I've always tried to be a very clear and precise writer, trying to reach the reader directly without having to go through the critic.

GABRIEL GARCIA MARQUEZ
In *Writers at Work, Sixth Series* (1984)

I can read the most devastating things about myself now and it doesn't make my pulse skip a beat. You know, the writer is inclined to be a sensitive person, and he can read 100 good reviews and one bad review and take that bad review to heart.

TRUMAN CAPOTE
In *On Being a Writer* (1989)

Critics are always going to pick a fight with one or another of your stories. Every review I've read or written has the "but" paragraph.

CHRISTOPHER TILGHMAN
In *Passion and Craft: Conversation with Notable Writers* (1998)

There is only one thing in the world worse than being talked about, and this is not being talked about.

Oscar Wilde
The Picture of Dorian Gray (1891)

It is not authors only who are killed by criticism but critics as well; they seem, like scorpions, able to destroy themselves with their own venom.

CYRIL CONNOLLY
Enemies of Promise (1938)

9

Journalism
and
Nonfiction

——•◦•——

The Facts and Beyond

Journalism, the mother to literature, will probably be a mother to you. I started out there. I've still got the bruises on my soul but how I learned! You get paid for your work in journalism—not well, but paid nonetheless . . . The competition is tough. You hustle or you starve.

RITA MAE BROWN
Starting from Scratch (1988)

It is right for a good man to love his friends and his country, and to hate the enemies of both. But when a man takes upon him to write history, he must throw aside all such feelings, and be prepared, on many occasions, to extol even an enemy, when his conduct deserves applause; nor should he hesitate to censure his dearest and most esteemed friends, whenever their deeds call for condemnation.

POLYBIUS

So let's establish between us that despite my pleas to authors to tell it like a story, there remain many devices of fictional storytelling that cannot be adapted to nonfiction writing. You cannot introduce made-up facts or dialogue, no matter how trivial.

SUSAN RABINER AND ALFRED FORTUNATO
Thinking Like Your Editor (2002)

What I've always wanted to do is to write the sort of book which fellow historians would have to take seriously, but which was really a book for the educated general reader who would like to be informed, to have his view of the world enlarged about a particular subject.

JOHN KEEGAN

In *Booknotes: America's Finest Authors on Reading, Writing, and the Power of Ideas* (1977)

Many remarkable writers not only survive immense amounts of hack work, they gain know-how from it.

CHRISTOPHER ISHERWOOD
In *Writers at Work, Fourth Series* (1976)

The only qualities essential for real success in journalism are ratlike cunning, a plausible manner, and a little literary ability . . . [and] . . . the capacity to steal other people's ideas and phrases—that one about ratlike cunning was invented by my colleague Murray Sayre—is also invaluable.

NICHOLAS TOMALIN, ENGLISH JOURNALIST
In *Poison Penmanship: The Gentle Art of Muckraking* (1979)

When *Time,* commenting in its press section on the Famous Writers School Fracas, called me "Queen of Muckrakers," I rushed to the dictionary to find out what I was queen of, and discovered that "muckracker" was originally a pejorative coined by President Theodore Roosevelt to describe journalists . . . [whom he felt had gone too far in their attempts to expose government and corporate corruption]

JESSICA MITFORD
Poison Penmanship: The Gentle Art of Muckraking (1979)
[MITFORD'S EXPOSÉ ON "THE FAMOUS WRITERS SCHOOL" IN
The Atlantic (1970) LED TO THE EVENTUAL COLLAPSE OF THE
SCHOOL AND ITS PUBLICLY HELD STOCK.]

People don't ask for facts in making up their minds. They would rather have one good, soul-satisfying emotion than a dozen facts.

ROBERT KEITH LEAVITT
Voyages and Discoveries (1939)

The writing of history was summed up by John Keats in ten words in a letter . . . He said: "A fact is not a truth until you love it." You have to become attached to the thing you're writing about—in other words, "love it"—for it to have any real meaning.

SHELBY FOOTE
In *Paris Review Interview* Number 151 (1951)

Every journalist has a novel in him, which is an excellent place for it.

RUSSELL LYNES, FORMER MANAGING EDITOR, *Harper's Magazine*
In *Quotations of Wit and Wisdom* (1975)

Most writers of fiction are superior to all but the best historians in characterization and description. If you have difficulty in making people and events seem real, see if you cannot learn the technique from American novelists such as Sherwood Anderson, Joseph Hergesheimer, and Margaret Mitchell.

SAMUEL ELIOT MORISON
In *Sailor Historian: The Best of Samuel Eliot Morison* (1977)

The best piece of advice I got . . . was from a colleague of mine, David Ignatius. . . . He said: " . . . always imagine whether the reader is going to want to turn the page. Whether what you're writing, how you're writing, and the anecdotes you're telling will compel the reader to turn the page."

THOMAS FRIEDMAN
In *Booknotes: America's Finest Authors on Reading, Writing, and the Power of Ideas* (1977)

If you steal from one author it's plagiarism; if you steal from many it's research.

WILSON MIZNER
In *The Legendary Mizners* (1953)

Autobiography is probably the most respectable form of lying.

HUMPHREY CARPENTER
"Patrick White Explains Himself", in *The New York Times Book Review* (February 7, 1982)

A columnist is not much more than a reporter with a point of view, and to the attitude one adds a touch of special flavor—if possibly, one's own flavor, even if it's a touch garlicky.

ROBERT RUARK
In *The Lost Classics of Robert Ruark* (1996)

The difference between journalism and literature is that journalism is unreadable and literature is not read.

OSCAR WILDE

The pen is mightier than the sword.

EDWARD GEORGE BULWER-LYTTON
Richelieu (1839)

Whether we are writing about murder trials, barrage balloons, spring flowers, or autumn colors, fake it not! Sticking to the facts . . . contributes to the integrity of whatever we're writing. And . . . fiction or non-fiction, in the end that is all we have to sell—the credibility and integrity of the words we put together.

James J. Kilpatrick
The Writer's Art (1984)

If news is treated like any other product being sold for money, then it will be made the way people like it. Newspapers will print what people want to read, not what they ought to know.

ANDREW J. ROONEY
Pieces of My Mind (1982)

I was influenced in my writing very much by Truman Capote's book *In Cold Blood.* He made me realize that ... a book could have the narrative drive of a novel and yet could be about real events, which are often much more interesting than those that appear in a novel.

NEIL SHEEHAN

In *Booknotes: America's Finest Authors on Reading, Writing, and the Power of Ideas* (1977)

I was one of many who began to experiment, early on, with ways of using the device of fiction in journalism. . . . It . . . has opened up journalism a lot. . . . The fictional mode made it easier for the reader to imagine that these events were happening to him.

JOHN HERSEY
In *Writers at Work: The Paris Review Interviews,*
Eighth Series (1988)

Reporting . . . can be accurate, like a photograph taken . . . to record. The best of nonfiction, however, often sets what it sees in a framework, what has happened elsewhere or in the past. As the recorded events march before the reader, a scrim lifts to convey other dimensions, sight becomes insight, reporting becomes art.

SOL STEIN
Stein on Writing (1995)

The columnist tries to capture the color, flavor and electricity of an event. It's not an easy assignment.

RED SMITH
In *On Being a Writer* (1989)

Good reporting is expensive and hard. The reason . . . is that half the world is trying to hide the truth from the other half. Too many government officials, business executives, union leaders and ordinary citizens . . . are doing things they don't want anyone to know about, and they're good at concealing them.

ANDREW A. ROONEY
Word for Word (1986)

Obviously the novelist can take us into hidden places where no other writer can go . . . [But] I have no patience with the snobbery that accompanies "literature"—the snobbery which says that non-fiction is only journalism by another name, and that journalism by any name is a dirty word.

WILLIAM ZINSSER
On Writing Well: An Informal Guide to Writing Nonfiction (1980)

I think if I knew all about it [the subject of a new book] and I knew exactly what I was going to say, I probably wouldn't want to write the book, because there would be no search, there would be no exploration of a country I've never been to—that's the way one should feel.

DAVID MCCULLOUGH

In *Booknotes: America's Finest Authors on Reading, Writing, and the Power of Ideas* (1977)

My only advantage as reporter is that I am so physically small, so temperamentally unobtrusive, and so neurotically inarticulate that people tend to forget that my presence runs counter to their best interests. And it always does. That is one last thing to remember: *writers are always selling somebody out.*

JOAN DIDION
Preface, *Slouching Toward Bethlehem* (1968)

In my zeal to set the scene, I had the diamond-studded belt of Orion girdling the bare limbs of a mighty oak—only to be advised by a startled astronomer that on the night in question, Orion could not possibly have been where I put it.

JAMES J. KILPATRICK
The Writer's Art (1984)
[THE SAME SORT OF "ZEAL" TRIPPED UP NONE OTHER THAN ERNEST HEMINGWAY, WHO, IN *The Old Man and the Sea*, HAD HIS "OLD MAN" OBSERVE THE SOUTHERN CROSS IN ONE SCENE—IMPOSSIBLE AT THE TIME AND LATITUDE IN THE STORY, AND AS AN EXPERIENCED JOURNALIST, "PAPA" WAS SEVERELY EMBARRASSED BY THE ERROR.]

10

The Artistic Temperament

Take That!

A writer is somebody for whom writing is more difficult than it is for other people.

THOMAS MANN
Essays of Three Decades

———•••———

The truth is . . . no matter how many times I've tried to read *Don Quixote*, I've never been able to get beyond page six. Indeed, so soporific is its effect that I believe it should be withdrawn from libraries everywhere and dispensed only on prescription.

S. J. PERELMAN
The Last Laugh (1981)

All writers are vain, selfish and lazy, and at the very bottom of their motives lies a mystery.

GEORGE ORWELL
Collected Essays (1968)

Writers, you know, are the beggars of western society.

OCTAVIO PAZ
In *The Independent* (December 30, 1990)

Everyone thinks writers must know more about the inside of the human head, but that is wrong. They know less, that's why they write: trying to find out what everyone else takes for granted.

MARGARET ATWOOD
Dancing Girls and Other Stories (1982)

———

Each writer is born with a repertory company in his head.

GORE VIDAL
In *Dallas Times Herald* (June 18, 1978)

There is a splinter of ice in the heart of a writer.

GRAHAM GREENE
A Sort of Life (1971)
[GREENE DESCRIBING HIS FASCINATION WITH WITNESSING
THE DEATH OF A CHILD IN A HOSPITAL WHERE GREENE WAS
RECOVERING FROM APPENDICITIS.]

I know no person so perfectly disagreeable and even dangerous as an author.

KING WILLIAM IV

Writers live twice. They go along with their regular life ... But there's another part of them that they have been training. The one that lives everything a second time. That sits down and sees their life again and goes over it. Looks at the texture and details.

NATALIE GOLDBERG
Writing Down the Bones (1986)

———

Novelists, whatever else they may be besides, are also children talking to children—in the dark.

BERNARD DE VOTO
The World of Fiction (1950)

I have nothing to declare except my genius.

OSCAR WILDE
In *Oscar Wilde* (1918)
[REMARK AT THE NEW YORK CUSTOM HOUSE]

———

The most real thing for the writer is the life of the spirit, the growth or curve of vision within him of which he is the custodian, selecting the experiences propitious to its development, protecting it from those unfavourable. When he fails to do this something seems to rot . . .

CYRIL CONNOLLY
Enemies of Promise (1938)

You shouldn't pay very much attention to anything writers say. They don't know why they do what they do. They're like good tennis players or good painters, who are just full of nonsense, pompous and embarrassing . . .

JOHN BARTH
In *The Contemporary Writer* (1972)

Writers really take their worst shellacking from other writers.

E. B. WHITE
In *On Writing* (1990)

When a writer becomes the center of his attention, he has become a nudnick, and a nudnick who believes he is profound is worse than just a plain nudnick.

ISAAC BASHEVIS SINGER
In *The New York Times* (November 26, 1978)

It would seem that genius is of two kinds, one of which blazes up in youth and dies down, while the other matures, like Milton's or Goethe's . . . putting out new branches . . . The artist . . . may find himself exhausted by the sprint of youth and unfitted for the marathon of middle age.

CYRIL CONNOLLY
Enemies of Promise (1938)

Hemingway had many grievous faults but there was one thing he did not lack: artistic integrity. It shines like a beacon through his whole life. He set himself the task of creating a new way of writing English, and fiction, and he succeeded.

PAUL JOHNSON
Intellectuals (1988)

I don't think any novelist should be concerned with literature. Literature should be left to essayists.

JACQUELINE SUSANN
In *Lovely Me: The Life of Jacqueline Susann* (1987)

Beware of the scribes who like to go about in long robes, and love salutations in the market places . . . and the place of honor at feasts; who devour widows' houses . . . .

LUKE 20:46, 47
[BIBLICAL QUOTE USED BY JESSICA MITFORD TO LEAD OFF HER ARTICLE "LET US NOW PRAISE FAMOUS WRITERS," A DEVASTATING EXPOSE IN *The Atlantic Monthly* ON THE FAMOUS WRITERS SCHOOL, 1970.]

Literary *Schadenfreude*—one writer tearing down another's respectable work in the evident effort to build up his own—is evidence that the rule of professionalism has been broken.

GEORGE V. HIGGINS
On Writing (1990)

We have no great writers today, but we are certainly heavy on literary lightweights with delusions of grandeur.

ROBERT RUARK
In *The Lost Classics of Robert Ruark* (1996)

Remarks are not literature.

GERTRUDE STEIN
In *Hemingway: The Paris Years* (1989)
[COMMENT TO ERNEST HEMINGWAY AFTER READING AN EARLY
DRAFT OF "BIG TWO-HEARTED RIVER" IN WHICH HEMINGWAY
INCLUDED SEVERAL PASSAGES OF MEDITATION BY THE STORY'S
PROTAGONIST, NICK ADAMS. HEMINGWAY LATER DELETED THE
PASSAGES. THEY ARE, HOWEVER, INCLUDED IN *The Nick Adams
Stories*, EDITED BY PHILIP YOUNG.]

"Your novels just won't do, you know."

GEORGE BERNARD SHAW TO JOSEPH CONRAD
In *On Writing and the Novel* (1987)

Hemingway is certainly the better of the two; he has at least a voice of his own. . . . But I cannot abide Conrad's souvenir-shop style, and bottled ships, and shelled necklaces of romanticist clichés. . . . In mentality and emotion, they are hopelessly juvenile . . .

VLADIMIR NABOKOV
In *Playboy Interviews* (1967)

[Hemingway] applied the same strategies to every book, strategies as it happens that he came upon and invented quite early on in his career. They were his triumph in the early days. But by the last decade or two of his working life they trapped him, restricted him, and defeated him.

E. L. DOCTOROW
In *Writers at Work: The Paris Review Interviews, Eighth Series* (1988)

Don't tell us petty stories of our own pettiness. . . . Go back where there are temples and jungles and all manner of unknown things, where there are mountains whose summits have never been scaled, rivers whose sources have never been reached, deserts whose sands have never been crossed.

WILLA CATHER
[ADVICE TO RUDYARD KIPLING, WHO WAS LIVING IN VERMONT AT THE TIME.]

That's not writing, that's typing.

TRUMAN CAPOTE
In David Susskind interview (1959)
[CRITICIZING JACK KEROUAC'S *On the Road.*]

Not only did the huge first printing sell out [one million plus copies of *A Man in Full*] but so did seven subsequent editions of 25,000 each . . . Three big-name American novelists, heavy with age and literary prestige—John Updike, Norman Mailer, and John Irving—rose up to denounce *A Man in Full*.

TOM WOLFE
Hooking Up (2000)

Moby Dick is our most daring and our most thoroughly American work of prose fiction, a book of wonders yet to be—like its enigmatic whale—thoroughly comprehended.

JOYCE CAROL OATES
Woman Writer: Occasions and Opportunities (1988)

All of you young people who served in the war. You are a lost generation.

GERTRUDE STEIN

In *A Moveable Feast* (1964)

[HEMINGWAY USED THE QUOTE IN THE FRONTISPIECE OF HIS NOVEL *The Sun Also Rises*.]

This is not a novel to be tossed aside lightly. It should be thrown with great force.

DOROTHY PARKER
Wit's End (1973)

I think Americans, perhaps more than other people, are impressed by what they don't understand, and the poets take advantage of this. Gertrude Stein has had an amazing amount of newspaper space, out of all proportion to the pleasure she has given people by her writings, it seems to me

E. B. WHITE
One Man's Meat (1982)

Liking a writer (i.e., his work) and then meeting the writer is like liking pâté de fois gras and then meeting the goose.

ARTHUR KOESTLER, REMARK TO A FAN
In *World Literary Anecdotes* (1990)

Its characters are confusedly drawn and by their acts and words they prove that they are not the sort of people the author claims that they are; its humor is pathetic; its pathos is funny; its conversations are— oh! indescribable; its love-scenes odious; its English a crime against the language.

MARK TWAIN
In *The Portable Mark Twain* (1946)
[FROM HIS FAMOUS REVIEW OF *The Deerslayer*, "FENIMORE COOPER'S LITERARY OFFENSES."]

11

Literary Horizons

The Search for Excellence

I am convinced more and more day by day that fine writing is next to fine doing, the top thing in the world.

JOHN KEATS
Letter to J. H. Reynolds (1819)

Our task as we sit (or stand or lie) is to rise above the setting, with its comforts and distractions, into a relationship with our ideal reader, who wishes from us nothing but the fruit of our best instincts, more honest inklings, and firmest persuasions.

JOHN UPDIKE
Introduction, *The Writer's Desk* (1996)

The pen is the tongue of the mind.

MIGUEL DE CERVANTES

———•••———

I want . . . the full measure of a writer's heart . . . Then, too, I want a book so filled with story and character that I read page after page . . . crazed . . . with an unappeasable thirst to know what happens next.

PAT CONROY
In *Why I Write: Thoughts on the Craft of Fiction* (1998)

The story is primitive, it reaches back to the origins of literature, before reading was discovered, and it appeals to what is primitive in us. That is why we are so unreasonable over the stories we like, and so ready to bully those who like something else.

E. M. FORSTER
Aspects of the Novel (1927)

As a reader, I want a book to kidnap me into its world. Its world must make my so-called real world seem flimsy. Its world must lure me to return. When I close the book, I should feel bereft.

ERICA JONG
In *The Writer's Handbook* (1997)

The writer in Western civilization has become not a voice of his tribe, but of his individuality. This is a very narrow-minded situation.

AHARON APPELFELD

In youth men are apt to write more wisely than they really know or feel; and the remainder of life may be not idly spent in realizing and convincing themselves of the wisdom which they uttered long ago.

NATHANIEL HAWTHORNE
Preface, *The Snow Image* (1852)

Every writer hopes or boldly assumes that his life is in some sense exemplary, that the particular will turn out to be universal.

MARTIN AMIS
In *The Observer* (August 30, 1987)

There is no such thing as a moral or an immoral book. Books are well written, or badly written.

OSCAR WILDE
Preface, *The Picture of Dorian Gray* (1891)

All my life I've felt that there was something magical about people [writers] who could get into other people's minds and skin, who could take people like me out of ourselves and then take us back to ourselves. And you know what? I still do.

ANNE LAMOTT
Bird by Bird: Some Instructions on Writing and Life (1994)

Literature should be the work of clear-eyed men who take into account the totality of mankind. Literature has got to realize that it exists in a world where children die of hunger . . . that it lies within our power, as writers, and as human beings, to do something for others.

JEAN-PAUL SARTRE
In *Playboy Interviews* (1967)

The task of an American writer is not to describe the misgivings of a woman taken in adultery as she looks out of a window at the rain but to describe four hundred people under the light reaching for a foul ball. This is ceremony.

JOHN CHEEVER
The Journals (1963)

The American novel is dying, not of obsolescence, but of anorexia. It needs . . . *food.* It needs novelists with huge appetites and mighty, unslaked thirsts for . . . *America* . . . as she is right now . . . with the energy and verve . . .

TOM WOLFE
Hooking Up (2000)

What Napoleon could not do with his sword, I shall accomplish with the pen."

HONORÉ DE BALZAC
[NOTE WRITTEN UNDER A PICTURE OF NAPOLEON WHEN BALZAC QUIT HIS CLERK JOB FOR A WRITING CAREER IN 1819.]

Poetry is a purging of the world's poverty and change and evil and death.

WALLACE STEVENS
Opus Posthumous (1957)

The purpose of literature is to Delight. To create or endorse the Scholastic is a craven desire. It may yield a low-level self-satisfaction, but how can this compare with our joy at great, generous writing? . . . The schoolmaster's bad enough in the schoolroom; I prefer to keep him out of my bookshelf.

DAVID MAMET
In *Writers on Writing: Collected Essays from*
The New York Times (2001)

In great fiction we are moved by what happens, not by the whimpering or bawling of the writer's presentation of what happened. That is, in great fiction, we are moved by characters and events, not by the emotion of the person who happens to be telling the story.

JOHN GARDNER
The Art of Fiction (1983)

I do believe there is a level at which one can write where it is no longer a question of provoking or antagonizing, but simply a question of stating an overwhelming truth a man just cannot deny . . . After he has confronted the truth in that fashion, he is not the same man again.

ALAN PATON
In *The Writer Observed* (1956)

It is his [a writer's] privilege to help man endure by lifting his heart, by reminding him of the courage and honor and hope and pride and compassion and pity and sacrifice which have been the glory of the past.

WILLIAM FAULKNER
Nobel Prize speech (December 10, 1950)

A good writer always works at the impossible. There is another kind who pulls in his horizons, drops his mind as one lowers rifle sights.

JOHN STEINBECK
In *Writers at Work, Fourth Series* (1976)

A great book should leave you with many experiences, and slightly exhausted at the end. You live several lives while reading it.

WILLIAM STYRON
In *Writers at Work, First Series* (1958)

My task which I am trying to achieve is, by the power of the written word, to make you hear, to make you feel—it is, before all, to make you *see!*

JOSEPH CONRAD
Preface, *The Nigger of the Narcissus* (1897)

No literary form—the Shakespeare play, the epic poem, the Restoration comedy; the essay, the work of history—can continue for very long at the same pitch of inspiration. If every creative talent is always burning itself out, every literary form is always getting to the end of what it can do.

V. S. NAIPAUL
Reading and Writing: A Personal Account (2000)

My primary consideration is to *change*. I dare not use the word grow; there may or may not be growth involved . . . To still keep that openness, that chance taking-ness as part of the work. Not to be afraid to make a mistake, even if it's a long and costly mistake.

JAMES DICKEY
In *On Being a Writer* (1989)

The novel may stimulate you to think. It may satisfy your esthetic sense. It may arouse your moral emotions. But if it does not entertain you it is a bad novel.

W. SOMERSET MAUGHAM
Preface, *Cosmopolitans* (1923)

The bad end unhappily, the good unluckily. That is what tragedy means.

Tom Stoppard
Rosenkrantz and Guildenstern Are Dead (1967)

And there are three novels that I reread with pleasure and delight—three almost perfect novels . . . [*A High Wind in Jamaica* by Richard Hughes, *A Passage to India* by E. M. Forster, *To the Lighthouse* by Virginia Woolf]. . . . Every one of them begins with an apparently insoluble problem, and . . . you are going toward a goal. And that goal is the clearing up of disorder and confusion and wrong.

Katherine Anne Porter
In *Writers at Work, Second Series* (1965)

[What the story does] ... is to transform us from readers into listeners, to whom "a" voice speaks, the voice of the tribal narrator, squatting in the middle of the cave, and saying one thing after another until the audience falls asleep among their offal and bones.

E. M. FORSTER
Aspects of the Novel (1927)

A bad book is as much of a labor to write as a good one; it comes as sincerely from the author's soul.

ALDOUS HUXLEY
Point Counterpoint (1928)

All books are divisible into two classes: the books of the hour, and the books of all time.

JOHN RUSKIN
Sesame and Lilies (1865)

He [the artist] speaks to our capacity for delight and wonder, to the sense of mystery surrounding our lives; to our sense of pity, and beauty, and pain; to the latent feeling of fellowship with all creation. . . .

JOSEPH CONRAD
Preface, *The Nigger of the Narcissus* (1897)

But he [a writer] must go on writing, reflecting disorder, defeat, despair, should that be all he sees at the
moment, but ever searching for the elusive love, joy,
and hope—qualities which, as in the act of life itself,
are best when they have to be struggled for . . .

WILLIAM STYRON
In *Writers at Work: The Paris Review Interviews* (1990)

Works Cited

(also anthologies, literary reviews, and other sources)

A

Albee, Edward F.
in *The Saturday Review* (May 4, 1966)

Alvarez, Julia
in *Passion and Craft: Conversations with Notable Writers* (1998),
Bonnie Lyons and Bill Oliver, editors

Amis, Martin
in *The Observer* (August 30, 1987)

Angelou, Maya
Interview in *The New York Times* (January 20, 1993)

Appelbaum, Judith
How to Get Happily Published, Third Edition (1988)

Asimov, Isaac
How to Enjoy Writing (1987) by Janet and Isaac Asimov

Atwood, Margaret
Dancing Girls and Other Stories (1982)

Auden, W. H.
The Dyer's Hand (1962)

B

Barth, John
in *The Contemporary Writer* (1972), L. S. Dembo and Cyrena N. Pondrom, editors

Bass, Rick
in *Passion and Craft: Conversations with Notable Writers* (1998), Bonnie Lyons and Bill Oliver, editors

Bellow, Saul
in *The Contemporary Writer* (1972), L. S. Dembo and Cyrena N. Pondrom, editors

Benchley, Robert
Benchley Beside Himself (1943)

Bernard, André, editor
Rotten Rejections (1990)

Bernstein, Leonard S.
Getting Published: The Writer in the Combat Zone (1986)

Bickham, Jack M.
Writing and Selling Your Novel (1996)

Bishop, Jim
  in *New York Journal-American* (November 1957)

Block, Lawrence
  Telling Lies for Fun and Profit (1981)
  Writing the Novel: From Plot to Print (1979)

Blount, Roy, Jr.
  in *The Writer's Desk* (1996) by Jill Krementz

Bly, Robert W.
  Getting Your Book Published (1997)

Boswell, James
  Life of Johnson (1791)

Bowen, Elizabeth
  Collected Impressions (1950)

Bradbury, Ray
  Zen in the Art of Writing (1990)

Bradley, Marion Zimmer
  The Mists of Avalon (1982)

Braine, John
  Writing a Novel (1974)

Brown, Helen Gurley
The Writer's Rules (1998)

Brown, Rita Mae
Starting from Scratch (1988)

Buckley, William F. Jr.
The Complete Guide to Writing Fiction (1990) by Barnaby Conrad
and the Staff of the Santa Barbara Writers' Conference

Bulwer-Lytton, Edward George
Richelieu (1839)

Burgess, Anthony
The Agony and the Ego (1993)

Busch, Frederick
A Dangerous Profession (1998)

C

Capote, Truman
In Cold Blood (1966)
in David Susskind interview (1959)
On Being a Writer (1989), Bill Strickland, editor

Carpenter, Humphrey
"Patrick White Explains Himself", in *The New York Times Book Review* (February 7, 1982)

Carver, Raymond
Fires: Essays, Poems, Stories (1985)

Cervantes, Miguel de
Don Quixote (1605–1615)

Chandler, Raymond
in *Raymond Chandler Speaking* (1977), Dorothy Gardiner and
Katherine Sorley Walker, editors

Cheever, John
The Journals (1963)

Churchill, Winston
in *The New York Times Magazine* (November 13, 1949)

Clark, Mary Higgins
in *The Writing Life: Collection from Washington Post Book World*
(2003), Marie Arana, editor

Connolly, Cyril
Enemies of Promise (1938)

Conrad, Barnaby and the Staff of the Santa Barbara Writers' Conference
The Complete Guide to Writing Fiction (1990)

Conrad, Joseph
Preface, *The Nigger of the Narcissus* (1897)

Conroy, Pat
in *Why I Write: Thoughts on the Craft of Fiction* (1998), Will
Blythe, editor

Coonts, Stephen
Hunt for Red October (1984)
Flight of the Intruder (1986)
in *Writers Write: The Internet Writing Journal*
(January 2000)

Cooper, James Fenimore
The Deerslayer (1841)

Cornwell, Patricia
in *The Writing Life: Collection from Washington Post Book World*
(2003), Marie Arana, editor

Crichton, Michael
Travels (1988)

Crichton, Robert
in *Afterwords: Novelists on Their Novels* (1969), Thomas
McCormack, editor

Curtis, Richard
in *Honk if You're a Writer* (1992) by Arthur Plotnik

D

de Maupassant, Gustave
Preface, *Pierre et Jean* (1888)

De Voto, Bernard
The World of Fiction (1950)

Dial, Joan
in *Good Advice on Writing* (1992), William Safire and Leonard Safir, editors

Dickey, James
On Being a Writer (1989), Bill Strickland, editor

Didion, Joan
in *Women Writers at Work: The Paris Review Interviews* (1998), George Plimpton, editor
Slouching Toward Bethlehem (1968)

Dillard, Annie
Living in Fiction (1982)
The Writing Life (1989)

Doctorow, E. L.
in *Writers at Work: The Paris Review Interviews, Eighth Series* (1988), George Plimpton, editor

Dunne, John Gregory
Harp (1989)

E

Evans, Joni, publisher
in *The Writer's Rules* (1998) by Helen Gurley Brown

F

Faulkner, William
Faulkner in the University: Class Conferences at the University of Virginia (1957–58), Frederick L. Gwynn and Joseph Blotner, editors
Nobel Prize speech (December 10, 1950)
in *Writers at Work* (1958)

Fisher, Jennifer Sawyer, editor
in *Writers Write: The Internet Writing Journal* (April 1999), interview by Claire E. White

Fitzgerald, F. Scott
in *Beloved Infidel* (1959) by Sheilah Grahma and Gerold Frank
The Crack-Up (1945)
The Great Gatsby
Trimalchio: An Early Version of The Great Gatsby (2000), James L. W. West, III, editor

Flaubert, Gustave
advice to Guy de Maupassant
letter (1851)

letter to Ernest Freydeau (1860)
letter to Louise Colet (1852)
Madame Bovary (1857)

Fleming, Ian
in *Playboy Interviews* (1967)

Follett, Ken
A Dangerous Fortune (1993)
The Writer's Companion (1996)

Foote, Shelby
in *Paris Review Interview, Number 151,* (1951)

Ford, Richard
in *Passion and Craft: Conversations with Notable Writers* (1998),
Bonnie Lyons and Bill Oliver, editors

Forster, E. M.
Aspects of the Novel (1927)
A Passage to India (1924)

Frank, Anne
The Diary of a Young Girl (1958)

Friedman, Thomas
in *Booknotes: America's Finest Authors on Reading, Writing, and the
Power of Ideas* (1977), Brian Lamb, editor

Frost, Robert
Address at Milton Academy, Milton, Massachusetts (1935)

G

Galen, Russell
in *The Writer's Digest Handbook of Novel Writing* (1992), Tom
Clark, William Brohaugh, Bruce Woods, and Bill Strickland, editors

Gardner, Earle Stanley
in *Good Advice on Writing* (1992), William Safire and Leonard Safir,
editors

Gardner, John
The Art of Fiction (1983)
On Becoming a Novelist (1983)

Gibbon, Edward
The History of the Decline and Fall of the Roman Empire
(1776–1788)

Gide, André (1869–1951)
in *Woman Writer: Occasions and Opportunities* (1988) by Joyce
Carol Oates

Goethe, Johann Wolfgang von
Poetry and Truth (1811–1833)

Goldberg, Natalie
Thunder and Lightning: Cracking Open the Writer's Craft (2000)
Writing Down the Bones (1986)

Goldman, William
Adventures in the Screen Trade (1983)

Grafton, Sue
in *Snoopy's Guide to the Writing Life* (2002), Barnaby Conrad and Monte Schulz, editors

Greene, Graham
A Sort of Life (1971)

H
Hall, Oakley
The Art and Craft of Novel Writing (1989)

Hamilton, Ian
Writers in Hollywood (1990)

Hammer, Steve
interview with Tom Wolfe (1998), http://www.nuvo.net/hammer

Hampton, Christopher
in *Sun Times Magazine* (October 16, 1977)

Harris, F.
Oscar Wilde (1918)

Harrison, Jim
Off to the Side: A Memoir (2002)

Hawkes, John
in *The Contemporary Writer* (1972), L. S. Dembo and Cyrena N. Pondrom, editors

Hawthorne, Nathaniel
Preface, *The Snow Image* (1852)

Haycox, Ernest
Ernest Haycox (1996) by Stephen L. Tanner

Heffron, Jack
The Writer's Idea Book (2000)

Heggen, Tom
Mister Roberts (1946)

Heller, Joseph
Catch-22 (1961)
in *The Writer's Chapbook: The Paris Review Interviews* (1989), George Plimpton, editor

Hemingway, Ernest
Big Two-Hearted River (1925)
By-Line: Ernest Hemingway (1967)
Death in the Afternoon (1932)
Farewell to Arms (1929)
Green Hills of Africa (1935)
A Moveable Feast (1964)
The Nick Adams Stories (1972), Philip Young, editor
The Old Man and the Sea (1952)
The Sun Also Rises (1926)
in *Writers at Work, Second Series* (1965), George Plimpton, interviewer

Herman, Jeff, agent
in *Writers Write: The Internet Writing Journal* (February 2000)

Hersey, John W.
in *Writers at Work: The Paris Review Interviews, Eighth Series* (1988), George Plimpton, editor

Higgins, George V.
On Writing (1990)

Hughes, Richard
A High Wind in Jamaica (1949)

Hunter, Fred
in *The Writer's Handbook* (1997), Sylvia K. Burack, editor

Huxley, Aldous
Point Counterpoint (1928)

I

Irving, John
My Movie Business (1999)

Isherwood, Christopher
in *Writers at Work, Fourth Series* (1976)

J

Jackson, Charles
The Lost Weekend (1944)
in *The Writer Observed* (1956), Harvey Breit, editor

Jacobson, Mark
in *Why I Write: Thoughts on the Craft of Fiction* (1998), Will Blythe, editor

James, Henry
The Art of Fiction (1888)
Criticism (1893)

Johnson, Paul
Intellectuals (1988)

Johnson, Samuel
    in *Life of Johnson* (1791) by James Boswell
    in *Rotten Rejections* (1990), Andre Bernard, editor

Jones, James
    From Here to Eternity (1951)
    in *Writers at Work: The Paris Review Interviews, Third Series* (1967),
    Nelson W. Aldrich Jr., interviewer

Jong, Erica
    in *The Writer's Handbook* (1997), Sylvia K. Burack, editor

Jung, C. G.
    Memories, Dreams, Reflections (1961)

Just, Ward
    in *Writers on Writing: Collected Essays from* The New York Times
    (2001)

K
Kaplan, David Michael
    Revision: A Creative Approach to Writing and Rewriting Fiction
    (1997)

Keats, John (1795–1821)
    letter to John Taylor (1818)
    letter to J. H. Reynolds (1819)

Keegan, John
in *Booknotes: America's Finest Authors on Reading, Writing, and the Power of Ideas* (1977), Brian Lamb, editor

Kerouac, Jack
On the Road (1957)

Kerr, Walter
in *The New York Times* (1996)

Kilpatrick, James J.
The Writer's Art (1984)

King, Larry L.
The Best Little Whorehouse in Texas (1977)
None but a Blockhead (1986)

King, Stephen
On Writing (2000)
Salem's Lot (1975)

Koch, Stephen
The Modern Library Writer's Workshop: A Guide to the Craft of Fiction (2003)

Koestler, Arthur
in *World Literary Anecdotes* (1990), Robert Hendrickson, editor

Koontz, Dean R.
in *The Writer's Digest Handbook of Novel Writing* (1992), Tom
Clark, William Brohaugh, Bruce Woods, and Bill Strickland, editors
Writing Popular Fiction (1972)

Korda, Michael, publisher
Another Life (1999)
in *The Writing Life: Collection from Washington Post Book World*
(2003), Marie Arana, editor

Krementz, Jill
The Writer's Desk (1996)

L
Lamott, Anne
Bird by Bird: Some Instructions on Writing and Life (1994)

Lardner, Ring
Preface, *How to Write Short Stories* (1924)

Le Carré, John
in *The Modern Library Writer's Workshop* (2003)

Leavitt, Robert Keith
Voyages and Discoveries (1939)

Leonard, Elmore
in *Snoopy's Guide to the Writing Life* (2002), Barnaby Conrad and
Monte Schulz, editors

Levi, Primo
The Drowned and the Saved (1988)

Lipsett, Suzanne
Surviving a Writer's Life (1994)

Llosa, Mario Vargas
Letters to a Young Novelist (1997)
Interview in *The Paris Review* (Issue 116, 1990)

Lockridge, Ross
Raintree County (1948)

Lowell, James Russell
A Fable for Critics (1848)

Lubbock, Percy
The Craft of Fiction (1921)

Ludlum, Robert
in *Writing the Novel: From Plot to Print* (1979) by Lawrence Block

Luke, Prophet
The Book of Luke 20: 46, 47

Lustbader, Eric Van
in *Writers Write: The Internet Writing Journal* (July 2001), interview by Claire E. White

Lynes, Russell
in *Quotations of Wit and Wisdom* (1975), John W. Gardner and Francesca Gardner Reese, editors

Lyons, Nick, publisher
"No, No, a Thousand Times No", in *The New York Times Book Review* (July 26, 1992)

M

Macaulay, Thomas Babington
Macaulay: Prose and Poetry (1952)

Mailer, Norman
The Spooky Art (2003)

Malamud, Bernard
in *Writers at Work, Sixth Series* (1984), George Plimpton, editor

Mamet, David
in *Writers on Writing: Collected Essays from* The New York Times (2001)

Manckiewicz, Joseph
in *Writers in Hollywood* (1990) by Ian Hamilton

Mann, Thomas
Essays of Three Decades (1947)

Marquez, Gabriel Garcia
in *Writers at Work, Sixth Series* (1984), George Plimpton, editor
in *The Writer's Chapbook: The Paris Review Interviews* (1989),
George Plimpton, editor

Marquis, Don
Sun Dial Time (1936)

Marshall, Evan, agent, editor, and publisher
The Marshall Plan for Novel Writing (1998)
in *Writers Write: The Internet Writing Journal* (September 1999),
interview by Claire E. White

Maugham, W. Somerset
Preface, *Cosmopolitans* (1923)
The Summing Up (1938)

McCullough, David
in *Booknotes: America's Finest Authors on Reading, Writing, and the
Power of Ideas* (1977), Brian Lamb, editor

McGuane, Thomas
The Complete Guide to Writing Fiction (1990), by Barnaby Conrad
and the Staff of the Santa Barbara Writers' Conference

McInerney, Jay
  Brightness Falls (1992)
  in *On Being a Writer* (1989), Bill Strickland, editor

McKee, Robert
  Story (1997)

McMurtry, Larry
  Flim Flam: Essays on Hollywood (1987)

Melville, Herman
  Moby Dick (1851)

Menand, Louis
  in *The New Yorker* (December 1, 2003)

Mencken, H. L.
  Minority Report (1956)

Michener, James
  in *The Observer* (November 26, 1989)

Miller, Henry
  "When I Reach for My Revolver" (1955)

Miller, Sue
  "Long Story Short", in *The New York Times Book Review*
  (November 2, 2003)

Mitchell, Margaret
Gone with the Wind (1936)

Mitford, Jessica
in *The Atlantic Monthly* (July 1970)
Poison Penmanship: The Gentle Art of Muckraking (1979)

Mizner, Wilson
The Legendary Mizners (1953) by Alva Johnson

Morison, Samuel Eliot
in *Sailor Historian: The Best of Samuel Eliot Morison* (1977), Emily Morison Beck, editor

Morris, Wright
in *Afterwords: Novelists on Their Novels* (1969), Thomas McCormack, editor

Morrison, Toni
Beloved (1987)
Jazz (1992)
in *Women Writers at Work: The Paris Review Interviews* (1998), George Plimpton, editor

N

Nabokov, Vladimir
in *Playboy Interviews* (1967)
in *Writers at Work, Fourth Series* (1976)

Naipaul, V. S.
Reading and Writing: A Personal Account (2000)

Nathan, Robert
The Writer Observed (1956), Harvey Breit, editor

Nova, Craig
Brook Trout and the Writing Life (1999)
in *The Writing Life: Collection from Washington Post Book World* (2003), Marie Arana, editor

O

Oates, Joyce Carol
in *Women Writers at Work: The Paris Review Interviews* (1998), George Plimpton, editor
Woman Writer: Occasions and Opportunities (1988)

Obstfeld, Raymond
in *The Writer's Digest Handbook of Novel Writing* (1992), Tom Clark, William Brohaugh, Bruce Woods, and Bill Strickland, editors

O'Connor, Flannery
in *How to Get Happily Published, Third Edition* (1988) by Judith Appelbaum
Mystery and Manners (1969), Robert and Sally Fitzgerald, editors
in *The Writer's Craft* (1974), John Hersey, editor

Ogilvie, David
  Confessions of an Advertising Man (1972)

O'Hara, John
  John O'Hara on Writers and Writing (1977), Matthew J. Bruccoli, editor
  in *The New York Times Book Review* (January 6, 1985)

O'Neill, Eugene
  in *American Literary Anecdotes* (1990), Robert Hendrickson, editor

Orwell, George
  Collected Essays (1968)

P

Parker, Dorothy
  Wit's End (1973)
  in *Writers at Work* (1958), Malcolm Cowley, editor
  in *Writers in Hollywood* (1990) by Ian Hamilton

Parker, T. Jefferson
  in *The Writer's Handbook* (1997), Sylvia K. Burack, editor
  in *Writers Write: The Internet Writing Journal* (April 2003)

Pascal, Blaise
  Pensées (1670)

Paton, Alan
in *The Writer Observed* (1956), Harvey Breit, editor

Paz, Octavio
in *The Independent* (December 30, 1990)

Perelman, S. J.
The Last Laugh (1981)

Perkins, Maxwell, editor
in *Max Perkins: Editor of Genius* (1978) by A. Scott Berg

Petievich, Gerald
in *The Writer's Digest Handbook of Novel Writing* (1992), Tom
Clark, William Brohaugh, Bruce Woods, and Bill Strickland, editors

Plath, Sylvia
The Bell Jar (1963)

Plotnik, Arthur
Honk if You're a Writer (1992)

Podhoretz, Norman
Making It (1967)

Pope, Alexander
An Essay on Criticism (1711)

Porter, Katharine Anne
in *Writers at Work, Second Series* (1965), Barbara Thompson, interviewer

Pound, Ezra
The ABCs of Reading (1934)

Poynter, Dan
in *Getting Your Book Published* (1997) by Robert Bly

Price, Richard
"Writers on Writing", in *The New York Times* (January 13, 2002)

Pritchett, V. S.
Preface, *Collected Stories* (1982)

Proulx, E. Annie
Introduction, *Best American Short Stories 1997*, E. Annie Proulx, John Edgar Wideman, and Katrina Kenison, editors

Puzo, Mario
The Dark Arena (1955)
The Fortunate Pilgrim (1965)
The Godfather (1969)
The Godfather Papers (1972)

R

Rabiner, Susan, and Alfred Fortunato
Thinking Like Your Editor (2002)

Rawson, Clayton
in *American Heritage: Dictionary of American Quotations* (1997),
Margaret Miner and Hugh Rawson, editors

Reynolds, Michael
Hemingway: The Paris Years (1989)

Rhodes, Richard
How to Write (1995)

Ritchie, James A.
in *The Writer's Handbook* (1997), Sylvia K. Burack, editor

Rooney, Andrew J.
Pieces of My Mind (1982)
Word for Word (1986)

Ross, Harold, editor
in *The Years with Ross* (1957) by James Thurber

Roth, Philip
  Deception (1990)
  The Facts (1988)

Ruark, Robert
  in *The Lost Classics of Robert Ruark* (1996), Jim Casada, editor

Rushdie, Salman
  in *The Independent* (February 4, 1990)

Ruskin, John
  Sesame and Lilies (1865)

S

Safire, William, and Leonard Safir, editors
  Good Advice on Writing (1992)

Salter, James
  in *Why I Write: Thoughts on the Craft of Fiction* (1998), Will Blythe, editor

Sartre, Jean-Paul
  in *Playboy Interviews* (1967)

Sayles, John
  Thinking in Pictures (1987)

Sayre, Nora
  in *Mademoiselle* magazine (March 1968)

Scott, Paul
  On Writing and the Novel (1987)

Seaman, Barbara
  Lovely Me: The Life of Jacqueline Susann (1987)

See, Carolyn
  Making a Literary Life: Advice for Writers and Other Dreamers (2002)

Shaw, George Bernard
  in *On Writing and the Novel* (1987) by Paul Scott

Shaw, Irwin
  in *Writers at Work, Fifth Series* (1981), George Plimpton, editor

Sheehan, Neil
  in *Booknotes: America's Finest Authors on Reading, Writing, and the Power of Ideas* (1977), Brian Lamb, editor

Simon, Neil
  Barefoot in the Park (1964)
  Come Blow Your Horn (1963)
  Rewrites (1996)
  The Star-Spangled Girl (1996)

Singer, Isaac Bashevis
  in *The New York Times* (November 26, 1978)

Smith, Logan Pearsall
  in *Good Advice on Writing* (1992), William Safire and Leonard Safir,
  editors

Smith, Martin Cruz
  Gorky Park (1981)

Smith, Red (1905–1982)
  in *On Being a Writer* (1989), Bill Strickland, editor

Steel, Danielle
  in *Snoopy's Guide to the Writing Life* (2002), Barnaby Conrad and
  Monte Schulz, editors

Stein, Gertrude
  in *Hemingway: The Paris Years* (1989) by Michael Reynolds
  in *A Moveable Feast* (1964) by Ernest Hemingway

Stein, Sol
  Stein on Writing (1995)

Steinbeck, John
East of Eden (1952)
Journal of a Novel: The East of Eden *Letters* (1969)
in *Writers at Work: The Paris Review Interviews , Fourth Series* (1976), George Plimpton, editor

Stevens, Wallace
Opus Posthumous (1957)

Stevenson, Adlai
The Stevenson Wit (1966)

Stone, Irving
Lust for Life (1934)

Stoppard, Tom
Rosenkrantz and Guildenstern Are Dead (1967)

Strunk, William, Jr., and E. B. White
The Elements of Style (1959)

Styron, William
in *Writers at Work: The Paris Review Interviews* (1990), George Plimpton, editor
in *Writers at Work: The Paris Review Interviews, Fifth Series* (1958), Malcolm Cowley, editor

Susann, Jacqueline
  in *Another Life* (1999) by Michael Korda
  in *Lovely Me: The Life of Jacqueline Susann* (1987) by Barbara Seaman
  The Love Machine (1969)
  Valley of the Dolls (1966)
  in *The Writing Life: Collection from Washington Post Book World* (2003), Marie Arana, editor

T

Thomas, Bill
  in *The Los Angeles Times* (January 13, 1991)

Thurber, James
  The Years with Ross (1957)

Tilghman, Christopher
  in *Passion and Craft: Conversations with Notable Writers* (1998), Bonnie Lyons and Bill Oliver, editors

Tolkin, Michael
  The Player (1988)

Tolstoy, Leo
  What Is Art? (1898)

Tomalin, Nicholas
in *Poison Penmanship: The Gentle Art of Muckraking* (1979) by
Jessica Mitford

Toole, John Kennedy
A Confederacy of Dunces (1980)

Tuchman, Barbara
in *Good Advice on Writing* (1992), William Safire and Leonard Safir,
editors

Turow, Scott
Presumed Innocent (1987)
in *Writers on Writing: Collected Essays from* The New York Times
(2001)

Twain, Mark
Adventures of Huckleberry Finn (1884)
letter to George Bainton (1888)
Life on the Mississippi (1883)
The Portable Mark Twain (1946), Bernard De Voto, editor
The Wit and Wisdom of Mark Twain (1987), Alex Ayres, editor

U
Updike, John
Introduction, *The Writer's Desk* (1996) by Jill Krementz

V

Vidal, Gore
  in *Dallas Times Herald* (June 18, 1978)

Vonnegut, Kurt, Jr.
  in *Writers at Work: Sixth Series* (1984), George Plimpton, editor
  in *Writers on Writing: Collected Essays The New York Times* (2001)

W

Wallace, Irving
  The Writing of One Novel (1968)

Welty, Eudora
  One Writer's Beginnings (1983)

Wetherell, W. D.
  North of Now (1998)

White, E. B.
  One Man's Meat (1982)
  in *On Writing* (1990) by George V. Higgins
  in *Writers at Work: the Paris Review Interviews, Eighth Series* (1988), George Plimpton, editor

White, E. B., and William Strunk, Jr.
  The Elements of Style (1959)

White, John
  Rejection (1982)

Wilde, Oscar
  The Importance of Being Earnest (1893)
  in *Oscar Wilde* (1918) by F. Harris
  The Picture of Dorian Gray (1891)

Williams, Tennessee
  A Streetcar Named Desire (1947)
  in *Writers at Work, Sixth Series* (1984), George Plimpton, editor

Wolfe, Thomas
  The Story of a Novel (1935)
  Of Time and the River (1935)

Wolfe, Tom
  Hooking Up (2000)
  in interview by Steve Hammer (1998), http://www.nuvo.net/hammer
  A Man in Full (1998)
  Mauve Gloves and Madmen, Clutter and Vine (1976)

Woodford, Jack
  Writer's Cramp (1953)

Woolf, Virginia
  Letter to Vita Sackville-West (1928)
  The Second Common Reader (1932)
  To the Lighthouse (1927)
  A Writer's Diary (1953)

Z

Zinsser, William
  On Writing Well: An Informal Guide to Writing Nonfiction (1980)

Author Index

(also editors, publishers, producers, and other publishing/film professionals)